ONLY
RECEIVE

ONLY RECEIVE

❧

NO BARRIERS
NO BOUNDARIES

by Michele Longo O'Donnell

LA VIDA PRESS
BOERNE, TEXAS

Library of Congress Cataloging
in Publication Data

ISBN 0-9814649-9-8   softcover

Published in 2010 by
La Vida Press
107 Scenic Loop Road

Other publications by
Michele Longo O'Donnell

Of Monkeys and Dragons: Freedom From Disease
The God That We've Created: The Basic Cause of All Disease
When the Wolf is at the Door: The Simplicity of Healing

*As always this is dedicated
to my sister and brother in-law.
I feel your love and support now,
as I always felt it when you walked among us.
The suffering you both endured
is one of my greatest motivations
to end such unlawful,
illegitimate human experiences...
and to awaken us all to what is available for us,
now and forever.*

TABLE OF CONTENTS

ACKNOWLEDGEMENTS

A deep and heartfelt gratitude to several who made this book a reality. To my daughter, Linda, who has mastered the English language and is faithful to correct my many grammatical and spelling errors: and who is such a source of inspiration and encouragement to me. To Lee, who has mastered the understanding of both my thoughts and my purpose, thank you for your editing and for being faithful to speak up when you both agreed or disagreed. Thanks for your many other projects that keep us motivated and fulfill so many of my desires that might never have come to pass without your untiring efforts. Thanks to Melissa who edited, put the finished work into book format, designed and restructured it until it was perfect, who so faithfully manages and oversees the whole clinic, whose encouragement knows no bounds, and who mostly manages me! Thanks to Phil who keeps all the details of Living Beyond Disease flowing and growing, who wears many hats and fulfills many needs.

What a team! Much love to you all.

SCRIPTURES

Deuteronomy 11:11 "For the land, which you go into to possess, is not as the land of Egypt...where you sowed much but reaped little...but the land which you go into to possess now is a land of hills and valleys, one which freely drinks water that flows from heaven. A land which the Lord your God cares for; the eyes of the Lord your God are always upon it, from the beginning of the year even unto the end of the year."
ONLY RECEIVE

Psalms 145:16 "You open your hand and satisfy the desire of every living thing."
ONLY RECEIVE

Matthew 5:45 "For he makes his sun to rise on both the evil and on the good and he sends rain on both the just and the unjust."
ONLY RECEIVE

INTRODUCTION

Since the beginning of recorded history mankind has confessed its need for a God for basic survival. We imagined a God for every need. A God for rain. A God for sun. A God for harvest, for prosperity, for protection, for health, for fertility, and for victory over our enemies. All this because we perceived ourselves to be under the unseen law of chance and no one is comfortable living under chance. We felt isolated and alone and a victim of whatever may appear. We imagined ourselves stuck in a life that we alone must make work, and we knew we couldn't. The Psalmist cried out, "I am a stranger in the earth. Hide not thy way from me."[1]

In time, God appeared to Abraham as One. One God, One Source for all needs, for all of life. And we gladly began to pursue that One God.

We created rules, procedures, formulas, many avenues and stepping stones to reach this enormously powerful, yet elusive Deity. If things didn't go as we desired we concluded that we somehow messed up, which led us to create even more ways and means to "please" God...to qualify for his love and care. Our prayers and our pleadings knew no end... as did our insecurities concerning our worthiness to gain his favor.

Unfortunately, this continues to this day.

But a new day has dawned on the horizon of men's souls. Now God reveals Himself as the very Life of us all, of all creation, from the least to the greatest. Now God has become to us our very essence, our breath, the beating of our hearts. Now the long pursuit is over, and here it is. How much closer could it be than our life? "For God has chosen to tabernacle in man."[2]

And now the craziest "awareness" of all is unfolding. It turns out that God has been the one pursuing us all along! It is Infinite Love Itself that has been calling your name, drawing you from what seemed like an eternity away, to his heart. The whole time, all the years and long nights of "seeking" God, and we discover that the entire motivation for desiring him has been from his heart, his desire for us, his intention to be revealed through us, as us. Every provision for this has been in place, it only remains for us to understand it, choose it and to receive it.

All the endless rules and "necessary qualifications" for a relationship with God, the sense of inadequacy and failure that often produced, we now discover were all man-made and so unnecessary. For "you have not chosen me, but I have chosen you."[3] "From the beginning of time you have been engraved in my heart."[4] "Since before the foundation of the world you have been safely hidden deep in my heart."[5] "Hid in Christ in God!"[6]

Was all that seeking and searching unnecessary then? No, not at all. All along the ground was being prepared for the eternal seed of the awareness of his Life as our Life. All along the veil of separation was being removed from the heart, that one day we might look in a mirror and realize the unspeakable Glory of God.

Personally I loved the process. I enjoyed the pursuit. I never got too bogged down in religions' many rules and procedures, do's and don'ts. So I never found myself drowning in the quicksand of personal failure. Even when I was sure I was failing, I was blessed to seek God from a sense of desire instead of fear. I could always sense the joy of God as I tripped along finding my way. He was my Shepherd, no matter what bushes or briers I might have found myself in. No matter what mud puddle I might have fallen into, he was there to carry me along until I found my footing again.

But, unfortunately, this is not so for most of the folks that I have met along the way. I find a fear of failing God in their hearts. I find a sense of almost paralyzing fear to look beyond the confines of the rigid paths they have forged out for themselves. They are afraid of "doing it wrong" and suffering the punishment of God. They are sure that if they fail or go the "wrong way" they will incur eternal wrath and judgment. *Yet it is this very imagination of God that brings about the pain and suffering.* "As you have spoken in my ears...so shall you experience."[7] When will we understand that we experience in this life according to our beliefs? The issues of life proceed from the hearts of men,[8] what we have been taught to believe. Not from an angry God. There is no angry God. The sufferings of mankind are a direct result of this very idea.

Jesus tells us a story in Matthew: Three men received gifts from their master. The first two felt the freedom from their master to spend, invest and use what he gave them. They did not fear failure because they did not fear their master. But the last man was so afraid of his *perception of his master's wrath* at failure that he hid what was given to him (truth and understanding) and never was able to receive more than he originally had. When the master asked him why he remained in the same state as at the first, he replied that he was afraid of the wrath and fury of his master. He, himself, by those very words, consigned himself to "outer darkness where there is only weeping and gnashing of teeth."[9] Not because God wanted it or chose it or did it to him. But because he could see nothing else and therefore that became his experience.

As our image of God is restored...by Divine Love alone...then and only then will we be able to rise above the sufferings and anguish we see all around us to the glorious liberty of the sons of God. The liberty to be free. Free to find the truth. Free to live in the truth. Free to realize God is the Spirit that freely flows through us and is our very life. Free to live out from that Divine Life without hesitation. Free to know that "no evil can come near to us."[10] That "no weapon formed against us can prosper."[11] Free to laugh at calamity as it comes for recognition. Free to allow ourselves the joy of living in the Kingdom of perpetual goodness. Free to receive all that God is, for "he is our possession and he is our inheritance."[12]

A new day is dawning where the Only Begotten Son, the manifestation of God, is revealed and it is found to be as much you as it is Jesus! All as One...in him, who came and revealed this to us and secured it for us. "For from him and through him and to him are all things."[13] Where all the self judgment and self condemnation is gone forever and we stand in him...holy, accepted, blameless, undefiled, faultless and wholly innocent.

We cannot be content to know these words alone. We will never really know this by reading it in a book or by hearing a teacher tell us. We must allow God to reveal this to each and every heart. We must know how to live these words. To be them.

But to get there, and then to live out from there we must first uncover the great lie. It must be exposed and seen to be the deceiver of the souls of men. The devil then is not a person, but a belief, a perception...the great lie!

By the grace of God this book will both uncover what has held us in such bondage and reveal what lies beneath. Such Light and Glory could not be forever hid!

CHAPTER ONE

THE GREAT AWAKENING

Can mankind live beyond the grasp of suffering and disease? Is it intended that we do this?

How can this come to be?

Several years ago I had the opportunity to visit Scotland for the first time. As a tourist I did the touristy thing and wandered from one medieval castle to another. I was horrified at the preservation of heads displayed on stakes, weapons and instruments of torture beyond my imagination. It amazed me that mankind had at one time not only dreamed these things up, but actually made them with the pride of a true craftsman and then used them! Where was their sense of humanity? Where was their mercy for fellow men? I expected to see a history of very primitive living conditions. I expected to see a history of a measure of lack of sanitation and aesthetics, but this threw me. Why did they display this with such pride? Simply to preserve their history? My days were filled with this and I so wished that I had chosen to visit the local pubs, getting to know the folks who lived in such beauty and simplicity.

For Scotland was beautiful beyond my ability to describe. The rolling hills of deep green with specks of white sheep dotted against the background. The air was fresh and clean, quite invigorating. It made me want to run through those meadows until I collapsed. But instead, off we went to another gruesome memory of man's brutality to man. From there we dropped down to England to fly home, spending one more day in this arena at the Tower of London. Was this worse than what I saw in Scotland? It was hard to tell.

On the flight home I sat in silence as I reflected upon what was so heavy on my heart. My, but we have come a long way from those days and that "thought" that dominated mankind! Today we would be paralyzed at such horror. We would never stand for it. Our main concern now in the treatment of "enemy combatants" or criminals is that we maintain humane and dignified and clean surroundings for the duration of their incarceration. What a contrast! How far civilization has progressed! Today we look back at those times and think, "What were they thinking?"

Then my mind wandered to my favorite imagination, of a world devoid of disease and suffering, a thought that has occupied and dominated my life entirely since I was 17 years old. There is no doubt in my mind that this will be the state of affairs one day. No doubt at all. Soon man will have enough understanding and depth of wisdom to reject such nonsense as disease. One day we will have enough love and respect for the bodies we occupy that we will stop creating such imaginations of torture. Soon we will know the true nature of God to be mercy and love and incapable of creating something that could fall into such disrepair. We will know God as Love Itself and cease to feel worthy of such pain and tragedy. We will cease to build shrines to these diseases, in our minds and in our cities, which only advance the long endless and distorted conditions we have created. We have thousands of names of diseases, thousands of descriptions, prognoses, treatments and new ones being "identified" (imagined) each month. We have been totally immersed in this atmosphere of thought until our only concern is how to treat each appearance, having enough insurance to cover the growing and insane costs of treatments, how to live with this condition, etc.

We are beyond mesmerized, beyond hypnotized by these imaginations of fear until we are unable to realize that it is we who have invented all this...to our own destruction. If we can imagine it, we can experience it. We analyze each disease. We study it, dissect it, bisect it, resect it, until it is so entrenched in the mind that we are blinded to what we have done and are continuing to do. We swat at flies (various diseases) only to leave the pile of cow manure (images and beliefs) that continues to attract the flies.

We are filled with these images everyday, everywhere we turn, thanks to the greed for gain of the pharmaceutical companies who promote this information of insanity. They play on our fears. They capitalize on our imagination to create. And if we don't create it they create it for us. The more we allow such horror to dominate our thought and expectation, the more they gain.

My precious brother made his living selling pharmaceutical drugs, chemical poisons that only diminish our ability to resist further disease experiences. Many years ago as he was about to retire, he told me they "were going public" with their drugs. They were going to flood the airways, magazines and daily news until the people were thoroughly educated. I asked him why, and he said for marketing purposes. That it would make the people insist that their doctors prescribe more of them. It would make them more aware of the possibilities of things going wrong with their bodies, self-diagnosing, increasing fear of the body...as if we are not afraid enough of our bodies already! He said it was a "whole new way" of peddling the drugs. Instead of convincing the doctors to use them, how much easier to convince the public that they need them.

We are obsessed with disease and our bodies. We are so self absorbed by fear and horrible imaginations of impending doom, it has dominated the entire human thought. Billions of dollars are being sunk into new medical complexes, medical schools, and drug companies. So they won! More diseases are being "identified" every day. If we can "think it" we will experience it! It is a miserable tidal wave, a tsunami of shocking proportions, and man just keeps on marching to their pipe, falling headlong off the cliff to their own destruction. Generations will look back at all this and declare, "What were they thinking?"
When I contrast this with how man is really created, the Divine beauty, order, harmony, strength and dominion over

such destruction...I shudder at the scene before me. Have they not read, do they not know that they are made in the image of an Eternal Creator, who is indestructible, incorruptible, uninterruptible and perfect?

"God has made man to walk 'upright' before him..." The word *upright* here means to walk "as a prince in beauty and authority." It goes on to say, "But alas! Man has sought out many evil imaginations!"[1] Disease is but one of these evil imaginations we have created out from the ignorance and fear of the unenlightened mind. To awaken from this is to be healed. Just as I wondered on that long flight back home from Europe, "What were they thinking?" Even so will men look back at this time. They will read about the wild horrors we created, the pollutants, chemicals, toxins, and poisonous drugs we poured into our innocent bodies. They will stand aghast at the mutilating surgeries we paid people to do to us. They will wonder, they will ask, "What on earth were they thinking?"

Disease is an illegitimate experience. It has no creator, no eternal law to support it. It is from beginning to end a result of our thinking. It has no right to inflict, to dominate. It has no intelligence, no power, and no substance at all except what we give it. If and when we choose to stop giving it such powers, it will cease to exist. Like a hot air balloon that lost its source of power, it will fall to the ground.

Where then did this all start? How did this begin and what causes us to give it such substance and power? It is imperative that we look at this long and hard in order to realize the simplicity of walking away from it. This monster, this dragon that causes us to tremble in fear will be found to be as nothing. Isaiah 14:16 says that the day will come when we will look at this and declare, "Was it *this only* that caused men to tremble in fear, that destroyed the nations?" It is a matter of awakening only. It is a moment of sudden realization. Until that time men will fight, and insist on its reality and its power to destroy. "What on earth are we thinking?"

I read of a man who traveled to London at the turn of the 19th century, desiring that during his visit he would be able to see a hypnotist. He was an observer in the audience as he watched a man called out from the crowd to be hypnotized. This man was told that he was to eat the carrots which were in a barrel before him. So he ate frantically as the audience watched in horror, because what they realized was that it wasn't a barrel of carrots at all, but a barrel of feathers! Soon they were on their feet yelling at the hypnotist to stop him. They were so concerned for the life of the poor hypnotized man, stuffing his stomach with feathers. Finally the hypnotist silenced the crowd, "Do you want me to awaken him" he asked? "Yes! Yes!" The crowd shouted back. He answered, "Then let me awaken you all!" In a moment everyone in the room saw that he had not been eating feathers... or even carrots for that matter. He had not been eating at all! Both the sufferer and those that stand by in horror at the affliction are in a state of self deluded darkness.

When I was a teen I was required in school to read a best seller entitled, *Brave New World* by Aldous Huxley. It was a gruesome report of a world dominated by a hypnotic level of consciousness. Mankind was under the "spell" of a drug called "soma." They did as they were told without question. They believed as it was instructed they should believe, without question. They wandered aimlessly throughout their lives, shuffling from one experience to another, never really living at all. Was this author a prophet! I wondered how man could get to that place of total domination...never realizing at the time that it was upon us all already.

To repeat a story I have previously written about, once I received a phone call from a very distraught grandmother of a four year old boy. This little one had been diagnosed with a recurrent, malignant brain tumor. A year ago or so he had one surgically removed, but now, as they all feared, it had returned. He was on his way to be operated on again. She said they were going to stop along the way to repeat the MRI scan to be sure of the location and size of the tumor and wanted me to pray that the MRI would be clear. I told her that I could not pray that way because I would be agreeing with the whole picture to start with. The tests don't tell the story, the truth tells the only story that needs to be told.

This is what we all try to do. First we agree to something that God doesn't even acknowledge as part of his creation to begin with...then we ask him, who never created such a thing, to remove it! But I did tell her I would pray.

My heart twisted inside of me as I thought of what that poor little fellow had gone through and what lay ahead for him. Then it occurred to me that just that fast, I too, had been pulled into believing the picture before us all. So I stopped such a train of thought and began to talk to the boy.

His name was Brandon. I told him that I was sorry for all the words that had been spoken over him, words of disease, of suffering and death. I apologized for all the words spoken about such a thought as "brain tumor" throughout the whole world. For every word written, for every lecture given, for every person hearing the lecture, for every operation performed, for every drug invented having to do with this idea. I said I was sorry for every person told that they had such a phenomena, and every person who ever said it. I was sorry that we, the Holy and perfect Son of God, created in the magnitude and Glory of God, could or would ever be ensnared into thinking and believing such malignant ideas of destruction. I asked him to forgive me as I stood in behalf of all of mankind. I thanked him for his forgiving spirit and I told him that I, we all, loved him with the love that God had for him. The whole experience took about 45 minutes. When it was over I went about my day, not thinking of it again. Several days later the grandmother called to tell me that the MRI was clear indeed! And therefore the child was safe at home again. Later she, the child's mother, aunt and sister came to our annual retreat here in Texas and introduced themselves. Brandon was doing fine, but by mistake I had heard he was 4 years old and now they told me he was 24 and had a 4 year old child. We hear what we hear, don't we?

What happened here? It only takes one person who is awakened to see the truth to influence the whole. Just as it took only one person who is still under the influence of the blind hysteria to influence the whole, so it takes only one to awaken the whole. On one level of awareness we are all ONE. For there is only *ONE* manifestation of the whole of the Divine. The book of Romans says that by only one, sin and suffering entered the world, so also by *ONE* it is removed... and the truth of the beauty of all of creation is seen.[2]

A long time ago I was reading in the Old Testament about the dedication of the Temple built during Solomon's day. It was a grand and glorious event as Solomon spread his hands open to God before the people to dedicate the Temple to God. Among other things he prayed... that if God's people fell into the hands of their enemies and they were suffering under the tyranny of such oppression...if *only one person*, or if all of Israel, were to look to heaven (truth) and to declare it...would God free the people and heal their land?"[3] This he prayed several times during that one prayer. Think of it! If only one person saw the truth and with conviction declared it, would God hear and relieve the suffering? The Israelites had thousands of altars built for this event and thousands of dead oxen waiting for the fires to be lit to sacrifice, as was their custom. At the end of Solomon's prayer, the "fire came down from God and consumed the sacrifices!"[4] I would say that was a sure "Yes!" As I read that over and over, I determined to be that one person for all of creation to be free. I was so sure I heard the same "Yes!" An eternal resounding "yes!" for all of us to respond to! *For any one of us qualify as that one person every time we stand in the gap for another, holding the pure truth of God in our hearts and in our words.*

At that same retreat there was another awakening. A relatively young woman stood up and declared that she had been healed of breast cancer during the weekend. Everyone clapped and rejoiced with her, but I noticed her family sitting with her looking at her so puzzled. A week later I received a phone call from this woman telling me her story. Three years previous to this she had a breast removed for cancer. Every three months she returned to have tests done to see if she was still clear. Just two weeks before the retreat she had a bone scan, MRI and PET scan done, as usual. Only this time the radiologist showed her many areas of returned disease, including a large tumor behind her heart. They insisted on starting her on their menagerie of drugs and radiations but she refused, saying she was going to attend a retreat soon and would wait till after that. Her family knew nothing of this new development, hence the bewildered look on their faces at the retreat.

She was now supposed to take those same films, the three scans, to her oncologist to see what he would do about the turn of events. She said she was so sure of her healing but now was beginning to feel fear, not knowing how to deal with this situation. I told her I would "hold the truth" for her and to call me when the appointment was completed. She didn't call for several days and when she finally did she was shrieking with excitement. She told me that the oncologist put up on his screen the films that she carried in with her -- the same films that showed the myriads of tumor growths -- only now they were clear of any abnormality! Nothing showed up as being wrong, and she never mentioned what she and the other doctors had seen just three weeks earlier.

What happened here? She woke up. The spell of hysterical fear and man-made imagery was broken during that retreat and she found herself to be just as God made her to be...whole, complete, and healthy. Nothing had ever changed. She entered an entirely new conscious awareness, and everyone concerned was affected by the glory of it.

"Whatsoever God had made shall be forever. Nothing can be added to it. Nor can anything be taken from it. And God does it so that man should stand in awe of him forever."[5] Not in awe of a disease. But in awe of him who knows no disease, but only the pure and perfect works of his hands.

So now we will together explore what gives this thing called human suffering such *seeming* power over men and what has been done to eliminate it from the earth.

Chapter Two

THE PROBLEM OF WORTH

I spent most of my early years asking Divine Wisdom why we suffer so much. What entitles disease to exercise such power over innocence? The more I learned of the *true* nature of God the more I became aware of the vast contrast between the concept of suffering and the immeasurable Love of God. Suffering is entirely contrary to the Love and Mercy of the Eternal Nature.

How could man, created in the beauty, order, intelligence and Wisdom of such a One actually ever experience pain, disease? For, "Of his fullness have we all received."[1] Eventually the answer came, "Because they think they can!"

"Why," I asked, "do they think they can?" "Because they think they deserve it."

I could accept that answer because when I look back over the 48 years I have taken care of sick people, I couldn't count the number of those in terrible anguish who said to me, "I know what I did to deserve this!" Or conversely, "I don't know what I did to deserve this!" Which is the very same thought...they think they earned it! Whether they understand how they did this or not, still this is man's conclusion to suffering. Which makes God the progenitor of such experience. Or at least One who could stop it but chooses not to.

Where did this come from and what can be done about it?

Several years ago I had an occasion to watch a TV show where a panel discussion was in progress. The question put to them was, "How do we get to heaven?" The panel was comprised of six people from six different "religious" ideologies. They had a Catholic priest, a Rabbi, a Doctor of the Koran representing the Islamic faith. Also represented was an evangelical Protestant minister, a minister of the "New Thought" movement (not to be confused with New Age) and an atheist.

The first person who was addressed with this question was the atheist. She said she didn't believe in heaven, so she was immediately disqualified from the discussion.

The second person was the minister of the "new thought" movement and she said some really powerful words. She said that God was only Love and so we were in Heaven whenever we were experiencing this Love. They looked at her sort of funny, kind of condescending, and moved on. This was an entirely foreign thought to all of them and they simply couldn't begin to grasp it. So they dismissed it.

The remainder of the hour was devoted to the remaining four. The Catholic priest said that you must be baptized and then live according to the ten commandments. The Protestant minister said that you must be "born again" and then live according to the teachings of Jesus. The Rabbi said that you must keep the law of Moses and live a righteous life. And the Islamic minister said exactly the same thing, you must keep the law and live a righteous life.

The host of the show was also Jewish, so he seemed somewhat nervous when he asked, "Well, what if you don't always live a righteous life?" And the Rabbi answered, "If you put all your good deeds on one side of the balance and your bad deeds on the other, whichever way the balance leans will be the determining factor."

All four said that suffering was God's way of purifying us to make us worthy of Heaven.

I thought, "Oh, my God, no wonder we are so confused and afraid." If our eternal future rests entirely upon us, as they strongly declared, we are all in trouble. The book of James says that if we break one law, we have broken the whole of the law.[2] Goodness! We are doomed! And then the only thing left for us is to fearfully look for the punishment and purification we certainly deserve.

So let's dissect what was said here:

1. It's up to us.
2. We must earn God's favor.
3. We must always be righteous.
4. If we fail, we must suffer to purge and purify our souls.
5. We must die to achieve Heaven.
6. The more pain, the more we gain.
7. Heaven is far away.

8. We are not now, in our present condition, worthy of Heaven. (The Catholic Priest even cited a place we could go to purify ourselves after we die to allow us to be worthy of Heaven)

9. Our whole eternal future depends on our worth.

And so this is religion.

Religion is man's attempt to understand God and to bridge the gap between God and man. Religion insists that there *is a gap* and we are the cause of this. Religion keeps us feeling unworthy, doomed, separate from God, and then creates ways and means for us to "get fixed" so God can bless us.

In my mind there is a world of difference between religion and true spirituality. A world of difference between man's view and God's view. Between Truth and "words without understanding."[3] Is this what Jesus meant when he said, "You make the truth of God of no effect by your doctrines and traditions"?[4]

The word "gospel" means "good news." There is not much good news in the present understandings at all.

If we derive our information about God, heaven, and our part in all this from religion, we will feel unworthy. We will have a perpetual sense of failure. We will feel that there is a *necessary cause* for suffering to make us worthy, and it comes from God. We will not be able to resist it with any degree of confidence. We will even unconsciously attract it. Who can resist the will of God? If this is all so necessary, then why do we thrash about trying to be free of it? If it will assure us Eternal Life in a state of paradise, then why not just go along with the agony and consider it justified?

One thing that the panel did agree upon was that Jesus came to teach men concerning God and that no man who ever lived was able to prove his words by his works, as Jesus did. And so we will go back to the teachings of Jesus about this because his is the clearest documentation that we have concerning the true purpose of God, the true Nature of God and the truth of the kingdom of God.

How do we live in that state? And when do we get to live in that paradise where there is no disease, no pain, no suffering or fear? Where there are no accidents, no tragedies or horrible things that we presently see? *We must transcend one atmosphere of thought into another atmosphere of thought*...into another place and space of thought. We must have our perception changed, for Jesus said that "According to your belief, so shall you experience."[5]

The word belief and faith are actually the same. I have found that faith does not refer to a sort of blind belief, a kind of hopeless/hopeful clinging belief that some faraway God will do something for me when I am in a desperate situation. That is all too often what people call faith. But all it is a kind of blind, hopeless/hopeful clinging belief...and not faith at all.

Faith is a clear understanding and an absolute conviction of belief. And that kind of certainty only comes by true understanding both of God and our relation to God. It is an expectancy of something because you fully understand. In the absence of this people place their faith in what others say or believe. This is very shaky ground.

"It is given unto you to know the mysteries of the kingdom of God."[6] How many times have we heard from the "blind leading the blind"[7] that we will understand when we "finally get to heaven?" Such nonsense keeps us in total confusion the entire time we are here. Do we think that God is delighted by our groping round in total darkness, bumping into every jagged corner we encounter?

No! What God says is that "My people perish for lack of understanding."[8] Proverbs says, "In all your getting, get understanding."[9] *We experience what we understand to be true.* If we don't like what we are experiencing it's time to go back to the blueprint and get the truth from the architect.

One night while I was still steeped in the same religious atmosphere of thought that I watched in horror that night on the TV show, I had a dream that would open my heart to change my entire understanding.

I dreamed that I was outside at night looking up into a "buttermilk" sky when the clouds opened up in a circle and a picture of a starving child appeared. I was there with a huge spoon in my hand filled to overflowing with food. I extended it to the child whose mouth was open in expectation of some much needed nourishment, when suddenly I yanked my hand away and the child died. This was repeated twice more until I could stand it no longer and I woke myself up. In horror I found myself across the room, sliding down the closet door onto the floor. I sat there with my heart pounding. "When, my God, have I ever done this to anyone?" I felt such despair.

I got up, dressed and went outside to walk in the rain in the dark night. I walked for two hours and during that time I realized that I was teaching sick and desperate folks out from the doctrines of men. I was not giving them the bread of life that their hearts were screaming for, but the well worn traditions of the elders... words without understanding... as Job so clearly describes it.

I had no idea what to do, where to go, or how to correct this. So for five years I stopped teaching, stopped reading and stopped talking to God. I decided to let God do the talking and be my only teacher. I would walk for at least four miles a day and just enjoy the goodness of the Presence of God and whatever he would say would be appreciated.

It was during this time that I really began to understand truth from the heart of God. Where before healings were random, frequent in appearance, but seemed to have no rhyme or reason as to why or when they would appear, now I was gaining the understanding that allowed me to expect that they would appear and why.

I felt like the patriarch Job. At the end of his ordeal of suffering at the hand of the religious thought of his day (which was pretty much what is still being taught) he realized that he had only heard of God, but really didn't know him at all. "So I covered my mouth and repented for that which I had spoken."[10] Once God had revealed his true nature to Job, he declared, "I have heard of you by the hearing of my ears only, but now my eyes see you as you truly are."[11]

I let go of the doctrines of men and moved out from one atmosphere of thought into another.

⌘

One of the reasons that Jesus came to earth was for us to understand that we can receive and enjoy the paradise of Heaven right here, right now. He told us that this Kingdom of Heaven was right here. "For the kingdom of God is within you even now."[12] "As in Heaven, so also on Earth."[13]

Incidentally, the word Heaven actually means universe. *Uni-* refers to one. *Verse* refers to a song. One song, in harmony with true pitch, bringing forth a clear and eternal symphony of perpetual Life. This is a song of joy, of order. It is a song of Love and Mercy and forgiveness and tenderness. It is ruled by truth. Truth known and spoken in a spirit of meekness and softness.

The reason he referred to it as a "Kingdom" is because it is ruled by a king. A righteous, holy, being of immense beauty and strength. One of eternal Wisdom and infinite understanding. And since you are found "in him," that King, my friend is you.

Jesus is referred to as the King of kings. That makes you a king as well. As you take your rightful place *in him*, in this Christ awareness or consciousness, you and he are *One Being*. For truly there is *only One* Son of God. "Behold my Beloved Son in whom I am well pleased[14]...my only begotten son."[15]

In John, chapter 17, Jesus prayed that we would come to understand this idea of ONENESS and learn to accept it and live in it. Ephesians says we were *"in him* since before the foundation of the world."[16] Colossians says, "We are complete *in him*."[17] 1Corinthians speaks of there being One Body and we all members of that one body.[18] Later we read that there is one body, one Spirit, one Mind, one Divine expression of one God and that expression is referred to as Christ.[19] Romans says we were *in him* when he was being baptized, crucified, buried and resurrected.[20]

The idea of there being only One Son, and we all a part of this, is throughout the entire Sacred Scripture. Yet we hear nothing about this from religion. Instead we are told we are separate, apart, a gap that cannot be bridged. This legitimizes suffering for we "need it" to get right with God.

Do we read the same Bible?

If we were *in him* when the entire "sin consciousness" was destroyed, buried and forever done away with, (Hebrews, chapters 8-10) what then are we being punished for? Why then do we need this pain and anguish? Can this really be a part of this pure and holy Kingdom that we live in? Do we accept it simply because we are told we must? What would happen if we just said "No!"? No more of this for I am forever "Hid in Christ in God."[21] No more of this for I am forever "the righteousness of God in Christ!"[22] Wouldn't I be exercising my rightful authority as king of this most holy Kingdom?

Proverbs says that "When a fool reigns in the city, (you are that city) the people mourn. But when a prince rules, the city rejoices."[23] It is time for us to stop being foolish by believing whatever is spoken, but to "drink water out of the well using *your own cistern*, and not another's."[24] It is time to learn the truth from the Source of all truth and not that which has been passed down from generations to our destruction. 1John said that "You have no need to be taught of men, for the anointing which you have received of him shall lead and guide you into all truth."[25]

We have been given the Spirit of Truth to teach us. Do we ask it for understanding? Or are we content to learn from others, and suffer untold consequences?

Where religion tells us that heaven is far away, Jesus says it is "at hand."[26] Where religion tells us that the way to gain heaven is to die, Jesus says that we can experience it now and we do this by "dying to self" and not physical death.[27] "Death to self" is choosing to live as though your life belongs to the Creator of it and not to you. You learn to live day by day, moment by moment, according to Love and not by selfishness, self love, self preservation, self interests, and self centeredness. "For your life is not your own."[28]

Life is not difficult if we take advantage of the Holy Spirit in our lives to teach us and guide us along the way. This begins with a desire to live according to the Divine Purpose for which we have been sent here.

It really is simply a choice. Once the choice is made, Grace takes over for us and carries us along this way. And what exactly is this thing we call Grace? It is the activity of the Spirit of God in the human condition. The opposite of this is "the efforts of man to obtain." It is critical that we realize this and never fall into the trap of trying to do it ourselves. It doesn't work that way. Infinite Love will do it for us if we but choose for this. When Love does it, it is easy, holy and productive. When man tries to do it himself, it becomes another religion. We should know by now that the efforts of religion to gain entrance into God's Heaven are futile, and even deadly. We live by Grace. Grace is the activity of the Spirit in, on and through our souls, our lives.

While religion tells us we must suffer to gain Heaven, Jesus says that the way to enter is to "repent."[29] The word, repent, here means to *think differently*. And this is exactly what we are doing now. We are choosing to think differently. We are choosing to live in the safety and confidence of the Kingdom of God right now. Then it can be said, "No weapon formed against you will prosper."[30] "Nothing shall be any means offend you."[31] "No evil shall come nigh your dwelling place."[32] "You shall not see evil any more in your days."[33] "Whatsoever you do shall prosper."[34]

The terrible problem of man continuing to attempt to "reach" God, or heaven, *by self-effort*, is that it has always ended in a sense of failure and it always will. We judge ourselves and we judge others as not achieving it. We cling to a sense of separateness from the goodness of God while we desperately desire it. Why? Because we know we haven't earned it. If we would make a choice right here, right now to stop *trying to earn it and simply accept it*, we would soon find what has eluded generations of mankind.

This sense of failure is called a spirit of condemnation, meaning self condemning. It has been with us since the "tree of knowledge of good and evil".[35] Then, as now, we are told not to indulge in listening to the continual "inner critic." This condemnation is also called the "accuser of the brethren."[36] That perpetual, nonstop voice reminding us of our failure. Our not ever doing it right. Making us judge every move, every action...and always telling us that we are wrong. This keeps us accepting suffering to "right our perpetual wrong." We cannot rise up in our authority in Christ and forbid its influence in our lives or the lives of our loved ones, because we think somehow we earned this mess. Or we need it to be purified. This is why condemnation is so deadly.

And this is why God said that when we partake of such self judgment "we shall surely die." This is the concept of "duality." This is when we entertain the idea of being both human and Divine. When we believe we are a "work in progress." When we see ourselves and others as having both the human mind of perpetual failure, and the Mind of Christ. Echoing throughout the ages we hear these Eternal Words, "In the day you eat of the tree (idea) of both good and evil, you shall surely die."[37] It is utter confusion. Death wears many faces. It can appear as the death of the unity of a family. It can appear as the death of joy, of dreams, hopes and aspirations. It can appear as the death of a friendship or marriage. It can appear as the death of strength and health.

To end this we must finally accept several things, not the least of which is that we are created pure, holy and safe in him. We are good, not bad. We are a result of pure goodness.

WE ARE INNOCENT. NOT GUILTY. "Now unto him who is able to keep you from falling. And to present you _faultless_ before the Presence of his Glory with exceeding joy."[38]

Daniel said that the realization of this was what saved him from the lions during his ordeal in the lion's den. "God sent his angels to shut the mouths of the lions in that INNOCENCY was found in me."[39] I am sure Daniel struggled with the same inner critic that we all do, but he learned to ignore it. He accepted his innate innocence, _not based upon anything he had done or not done._ Just because he knew that was the way he was created to be.

And he knew this...that this whole earth experience is God's from beginning to end. His job was to _receive the goodness of God._ It is the nature of God to be good to his creation. "He opens his hand and satisfies the desire of every living thing."[40] The flowers receive his goodness without question. The plants, trees, animals, insects, even the stars find that they remain in their respective orbits by grace and not by anything they have done. All creation receives from its Creator, the Source of all life...all except man, who insists that it is up to him to pull this whole thing off, and woe to him if he fails.

Man is innocent. Has always been and will always be. But man cannot accept this simply because it is said. Something needed to be done for man to enable him to accept this about himself...so let's go back to the Israelites of old and learn what their experience taught us.

CHAPTER THREE

THE ATONEMENT

Moses brought thousands of Israelites out of Egypt (symbolic of world thought or mortal consciousness) but they were confused, scattered and without direction, understanding or trust. Sound familiar? They had spent their lives in total darkness listening to the ranting and ravings of human insanity and defeat, bowed under the tyranny of evil and suffering. Now that they were freed from this, "What should we do now? What is the truth? How do we live? How should we think?"

God gave Moses the law to give structure and boundaries to his people. Just as a child needs external enforcement of structure, discipline and boundaries until he grows to maturity and realizes that it all dwells within him. At such a time, the necessity for laws and restraint fades away and we become a *law unto ourselves*. Now we don't harm others, not because the law says not to, but because we have developed to one who has internal restraint, and so we become our own law.

When we first begin to drive a car we learn all the traffic laws, given to maintain order and keep us from destroying ourselves and others. But as we grow and mature we learn to drive with an attitude of graciousness and unselfishness. We are more patient and loving. We really don't need the law anymore because we have become a law unto ourselves. Galatians tells us that the Mosaic Law was given as a "schoolmaster, a tutor, until Christ should be birthed in our hearts."[1]

Even living under God's holy law, the Israelites still felt separate from God and inferior and unworthy. They experienced defeat and despair within their souls. They lived in what the Bible calls *the sin consciousness*. This is not so much wrongdoing, but instead simply *living in an atmosphere of thought where we feel separated, judged, condemned*. The sin consciousness then is a general thought that rules the masses. In it man is always looking for the consequences of our perceived "wrongness." Sin is not what we do but what we feel. It always speaks of separation and failure. This consciousness is ruled by condemnation. If man feels condemned, then in his apparent defeat he is unable to come out from under the influence of such and remains in a sense of "wrong."

Sin is a feeling, an inner conviction of "wrongness." Transgression is what we do under the influence of such a thought.

Now God is above all else, Mercy. This Mercy, which is our God, saw the perpetual state of despair that their sense of separation from him caused, so he gave them physical, material laws of behavior which would bridge the gap they felt and enable them to feel close to him and to experience the joy and sense of belonging that he would have us all feel.

And when they failed to keep the law, he arranged for various animal sacrifices, whose death would carry away the sin and unworthiness they felt. Remember that living in a sense of perpetual self judgment (eating of the tree of the knowledge of right and wrong) always results in death.

They would go through a ritual where they would place upon the head of an animal all the sins they labored under, as well as the consequences of the sins, and then slay the animal. This would then free them to be holy (in consciousness) and accepted and loved by their God. *Now remember that it was the people who needed this. God never saw them unholy to start with.* Just as God does not see you or me unholy, but still we struggle with being able to accept this. It was the same for them.

Daily they offered sacrifices for sins (sin offering), sacrifices for total commitment to God (burnt offering), and sacrifices for a sense of oneness with God and with each other (peace offering).

Why slay these animals? Let's look at the nature of the various animals to understand this.

The ox is the burden bearer. When we slay the ox we are declaring that we have made a choice to do away with carrying our own burdens. We are done with feeling responsible for our lives. We are declaring that our life belongs to its Maker and not to ourselves. It is a declaration of total surrender.

The goat is stubborn. It does not heed the Shepherd's voice. It goes its own way looking to eat whatever it finds. A goat will eat anything. Once I was at a farm to pick up goat's milk for the clinic patients, when I returned to my car I found them munching on the chrome on the bumper! There is a scripture I think of here. "You have played the harlot with every stranger under every green tree."[2] The green tree speaks of whatever promises life to us. The stranger is listening to whatever voice is in the land at the time. And there are many! Jesus said that his sheep "hear his voice and no other voice will they follow."[3]

The turtledove was also often sacrificed. This is a promise to love God no matter the cost we encounter. If we are always looking at what might happen if we follow his voice, we will never be free to love. Love seeks not its own.

And the Lamb is the ultimate sacrifice. This is willingness to follow without restraint. This is total trust, as the sheep will follow the Shepherd "withersoever he goeth."[4] The sheep know that if they wander, their Shepherd will leave the 99 and search until he finds them.[5] He will bring them home, carrying them the whole way. They are loved and they know it! They don't question and they don't deny. They are safe, content and peaceful under the Love of Infinite love.

The symbolism of the sacrifices is phenomenal. What brilliance is the Mind and heart of our God!

Once a year the much anticipated Day of Atonement was given to them, truly a gift from God. The preparations went on for weeks. This was the day that all offenses were cancelled out as well as any judgment accrued by these offenses. All debts were forgiven. Nothing remained that could possibly allow them to feel separated from their God. Nothing could remain that could make them feel anything but loved and FREE!

Pursuing the meaning of Atonement we find it literally means the act of repentance, regrets, the desire for release of guilt and the need for a deep sense of purification. As this is accomplished we lose the invisible wall that separates us from feeling one with God, our Creator. Hence, the At-One-Ment. A moment of intense rapture, ecstasy, palpable stillness and peace. Just as a sincere apology to another will dissolve walls and barriers erected by shame and guilt.

How is this accomplished? Simply by the act of vicarious suffering for offenses. In this case the animals "took on" the transgressions, thus relieving the people from the weight of the offense as well as the fear of the repercussions that would certainly follow. Guilt magnetizes suffering. Guilt is not assuaged until the offender has experienced enough pain to allow it to be dissolved. The act of animal sacrifice satisfies this vicious circle.

The priests placed their hands upon the heads of the goats, thus transferring the sins of the people. The goats were slain by the thousands. The lambs were also slain as a symbol of their devotion. The oxen were slain, symbolizing the death of self or much spoken of *ego*.

What a day of joy and rejoicing this was! Debts were forever cancelled. Every man was free of all burdens. Everyone was healed.

Their enemies heard such triumphant gladness that they trembled at the sound. No enemies would dare to come near to attack. They were clearly under a covering that could not be penetrated. Nothing could hurt them. There was no point in trying!

But gradually it all wore off and at some point they sank back into the same pattern of sin and failure. Why? Because "The blood of bulls and goats could never make the people perfect as pertaining to the *conscience.*"[6] No matter how much they sacrificed, no matter how much they desired to know God, they yet felt stuck in their perception of unworthiness. Their consciousness was scarred by generations of lies they entertained about their inherent failures and insufficiencies. By age worn references to *original sin*, an insidious belief that man was not made in the image of his creator...pure, perfect, guiltless, innocent...but instead stained and separated at arrival! I have come to refer to this as the "big lie."

The consciousness of separation from God and from being his beloved was too strong. The sin could be wiped out. The consequences accrued could be eliminated. *But the consciousness that created the whole mess was still intact.* So by necessity the Atonement Sacrifice needed to be repeated year by year.

Something needed to be done to wipe the slate clean. Man needed to start over with a new heart, a new Spirit, a new conscious awareness. He needed a mind that never knew separation to start with. A heart that never felt wrong. A spirit that automatically walked in holiness and righteousness. A sense of being that was entirely comfortable with its innocence and sacredness.

A new creature, a new creation, a new identity was needed.

So Infinite Love appeared as Jesus and became the Eternal Sacrifice that would not only wipe away the sin, but re-establish the eternal connection between God and man... by *eliminating the whole mortal, human consciousness, and giving man a "new heart, a new spirit." A whole new identity!* The old concepts, the old ideas, the old self-image, self-loathing and depraved, was once and for ever done away with, dead and buried, never to reappear again.

Here are the immortal words of the new covenant. The new promise freely offered to us by the most loving, merciful God who wants us far more than we could ever want him.

"A new heart will I give you. A new Spirit put within you. And I will take away your stony heart. I will put my Spirit in you and you shall know that you are my people and I am your God. Your sense of failure will be remembered no more. No iniquity (transgression) will be imputed to you (laid to your account). You will walk before me in a new life. And your joy, no man, no circumstances, will be able to interrupt. All this will I do by my Spirit, by my grace. You will simply receive this."[7]

Now how did the death, burial, and resurrection of Jesus cause all this to happen?
Oneness.

Remember, we, the entire creation, was *in him* from before the foundation of the world. Therefore we were *in him* when he appeared to the earth. We were *in him* when he was baptized at the river Jordan. We were *in him* as he walked the dusty streets of Galilee, healing the sick and raising the dead. We were *in him* when the most profound words ever spoken came out from his surrendered heart. And we were *in him* at his greatest moment of agony and awful separation.

In him we died to the old. *In him* we buried once and for all the old offenses, ideas, thoughts and beliefs. *In him* we rose to a new life. "Seated in heaven, at the right hand of power."[8] "Though we have known each other after the flesh, now we know this no more. For we are now a *new creature in Christ.* All the old is passed away and all things are new. And all things are of God."[9] Clothed with a majesty unknown to the false mortal mind.

In the Mind of God we were literally in him...as one man...as one son...as one being. This is why we can say with conviction that the entire sin consciousness...the entire mortal identity...the fallen, failed consciousness is buried. All condemnation, all consequences for past or present offenses, darkened, confused beliefs, is eliminated. The slate is clean. We are free.

For years I had wondered what the significance of this sacrifice really was. People said that all the sins were taken away...but we still sinned. People said that all the consequences of all sin were done away with...but we still suffered, got sick and died from those sicknesses. So it was a mystery. I knew it had to be huge, whatever it really was.

And then one day while I was asking God about it, I heard, "You must receive it." Well, I thought that I already had, but what began to follow was so startling, so deep and life altering that I knew this was different. I began to spend time, a lot of time, just deliberately opening my heart to receive this. I thought, "What would it feel like if I felt forever holy, blameless, faultless?" What would it feel like if I knew that "All power in Heaven and Earth was really given to me?"[10] What would it be like to know that every word I spoke would be honored in Heaven as in Earth? What would it be like to know that every person I felt God leading me to pray for would actually be healed? What would life be like if I knew beyond a doubt that no evil would ever visit me again? I would be forever safe and free of any influence of evil. There would be nothing, absolutely nothing to ever fear again.

So it was this that I allowed myself to receive. I knew it was mine just for the choosing. So I chose. And I kept on choosing. I received, and I kept on receiving. Not very long after this I began to change. At least my thoughts, my assessments began to change. I felt alive and whole and really complete. I felt free.

I finally accepted the Atonement sacrifice. With understanding. And I find that I can't emphasize that sacrifice enough.

For my whole life I have tried to "do it right" and sometimes I seemed to do it right, but often times I must not have, judging from the reactions I would receive. Anyway I never felt right. Everyone says how "right" I have done "it" but I never felt that way. Once, someone I loved told me that I was a phony. I felt my heart crush inside of me. I thought, "Thank God *you* have never seen me that way. Thank God that my righteousness is not to be judged by man, but by God alone."

No man has the right to judge another man's heart. "To his own Master he stands or falls."[11] When we look to other people for their judgment of how we are "doing " we will find conflicting reports and none of them are of any significance. When we look to ourselves for a barometer of our success, we always find failure. So we look only to he who judges righteously.

And he declares our perfection, our innocence, our "rightness" based upon his understanding, his creating, and his grace. Above all, we are righteous based upon the holy truth of our oneness. One Son, one visible expression of the invisible God. "As he is in heaven, so are we on the earth."[12]

For millennia man has labored under what I have just described, thinking it all depended upon his individual ability to perform. Now Infinite Love in his indescribable Mercy has offered us a new heart, a new spirit, a new way. Now he does it all. This is living by grace. Our entire dependence is upon grace to work in and through us this Christ nature that we may find fulfillment in our divine purpose and contentment in our personal lives.

It is true that every belief system has an outcome. "As a man thinks in his heart, so is he."[13] And we have suffered for generations because this is true.

But now the whole picture has been altered. Now "your sins (aberrant beliefs) and iniquities (producing aberrant behavior) I WILL REMEMBER NO MORE."[14] In other words, the consequences that would normally come from these strange ideologies cannot legitimately attach themselves to us because now we are a new creature, with a new heart and a new Spirit and the outcome of all this is by grace alone.

Actually it will finally be seen that nothing is new at all. Only the "covering" of the mortal identity is removed and suddenly "all things become new."[15] "Now we look in a mirror and behold the Glory of God."[16]

Unenlightened people might think this is a cop-out. A license to do whatever. They may think that this can only lead to more sin and confusion. They think that without us suffering the consequences for transgression we will never live in love and peace. People need, they say, consequences to fear to keep them in line or disaster will rule.

Well, disaster already rules. For generations punishment and consequences have been applied to sin and man has not even slowed down. Crime, wars, divorce, parental abandonment, civil law suits, poverty, myriads of diseases...all this has not deterred man from continuing in his insanity.

But here is the truth: "By Mercy and Truth iniquity is purged."[17] By the Mercy of God he provided a way that the old nature (condemnation), with all its judgments of right and wrong, (tree of good and evil) with all its failure to live the Christ Life, (tree of one life) is crucified, died and buried. "It is finished."[18] It is "remembered no more."

And now we live *in him* a whole new life as a whole new creation...resurrected into Glory with him, in him. "The fullness of him that fills all and in all."[19]

And it's all by grace. All the work of the Eternal Mind, Wisdom, and Spirit.

And it is for all men, throughout all time. As it is for me. And as it is for you.

To enjoy the wonder of all this, all we have to do is choose it for ourselves, with understanding, and receive it, accept it. Stop trying to achieve, to do, to be. Forget it all and let him live his Life as you, through you and in you. Stop judging yourself and everyone else. Stop being afraid of others. And start choosing to love, choosing to live, choosing to trust this whole scenario.

This is such a far cry from what I heard that evening on the TV panel discussion that attributed the whole success of life to the efforts of man. Jew and Christian alike believe in the Atonement...but only in theory. Only in words. Only as a day to celebrate. But who actually receives it?

The realization and acceptance of this brings the Kingdom of Heaven into focus for all men right here, right now.

A world without hate, without war, without malicious competitiveness, without abandoned children, without poverty, without divorce, without disease. "Behold, I make all things new."[20]

All things truly are beautiful, in Divine Order and all things are of God, and no longer the result of unenlightened, strange beliefs dominated by failed human efforts.

Now instead of looking for all this "when man gets it right," let's know, accept, believe, and choose that it *now is.* We choose it. We accept it. Finally we are able to see what God has held in his Mind forever. Finally we are able to live in the Paradise he established for us "from before the foundation of the world."[21]

Healings of families can now appear. Healings of relationships can now appear. Healings of hearts can now appear. Healings of bodies can now appear. The "new heaven and the new earth"[22] is here among us now. The radiant Glory and indescribable beauty of creation is here now. You are a part of it. It is you.

CHAPTER FOUR

THE MERCY SEAT

It is said that when the sacrifice was completed, "The veil was torn apart"[1] and now the Mercy of God is revealed for all men to embrace for all time.

What does this mean?

To understand we must go back historically to the day when the children of Israel wandered through their wilderness experience.

Moses was directed by God to erect a very large tent,[2] a sacred place that the people could look to as a place of worship. In this tent were two rooms, one was called the Holy Place. The other was called the Holy of Holies. These two rooms were separated by a veil. Surrounding this tent was a very large, enclosed space referred to as the outer court.

The outer court was open to all the priesthood to offer sacrifices for the whole nation of Israel. But the rooms in the tent were off limits to the masses.

In the first room, the Holy Place, were three pieces

THE TABERNACLE

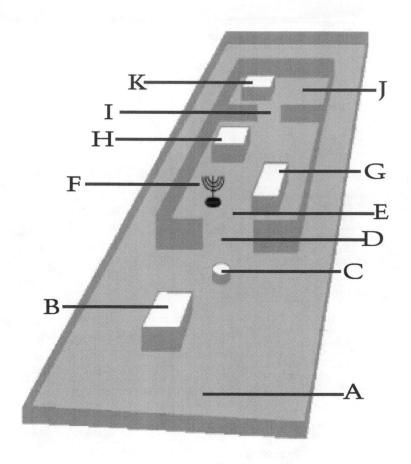

A--Courtyard

B --Altar of Burnt Offering   G --Table of Showbread

C--Laver   H --Incense Altar

D--Veil   I --Veil

E --Holy Place   J --Holy of Holies

F --Golden Candlestick   K --Ark of the Covenant

of furniture. One was called the Table of Showbread. Upon this table was placed blessed and holy bread. This will later be understood to signify the truths, the "bread" of understanding that men will partake of which will "lead and guide them into all truth."[3] These truths will "set them free"[4] from the confusion and darkness that dominated their experience. This is the "hidden mysteries of the kingdom of God"[5] that is exposed to all who truly commit their hearts to know and understand.

The second table had upon it a seven-pronged candlestick. This will be understood to signify the enlightenment that comes when the truth is known. Seven is the Biblical number for perfection. The truths spoken of here will cause men to understand their inherent perfection as created beings birthed from the Eternal Perfection of God. As the truths are increasingly understood the candlestick grows brighter and brighter. This is the only source of light in this room.

And the last piece of furniture was called the Table of Incense. This signified the prayers of adoration and worship offered to God through the days, the years and generations of mankind. As these are offered, the "sweet smell"[6] of incense rises up and over the top of the veil which separates the two rooms and the prayers reach the Mercy Seat within the last veil. This is the final sacrifice of all self interests.

The veil which separated the rooms was never to be breached. Only the High Priest could go into that space, and then only once a year on the Day of Atonement.

In this room was the Ark of the Covenant.[7] The

importance of the Ark of the Covenant to the Israelites cannot be measured. It was to them the Power and Presence of God. When the Ark was present they knew they were protected by God and nothing could breach that protection to do them harm. They were virtually indestructible, for God Himself was among them.

THE ARK OF
THE COVENANT

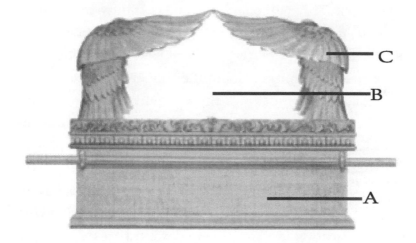

A --Ark
B --Mercy Seat
C --Cherubim

Within this Ark was contained the Ten Commandments, Aaron's rod of authority, and a pot of manna. Aaron was the first High Priest, even as we are appointed "kings and priests"[8] unto God. Aaron's rod speaks of the God-given authority each one of us has as priests unto our God. This authority over sin, disease, and all the manifestations of darkness and evil is never in question, never doubted.

Manna is the name given to the "bread"[9] that God provided daily for the children of Israel as they trekked through their desert days. It was found upon the ground each morning and gathered that same day. This is the daily truths, the daily word whereby the Spirit of God leads us to our "promised land."[10] A place of understanding and freedom from the bondage of failure and condemnation, into our rightful acceptance of being in and as his only begotten son! It is the assurance that we will be watched over and cared for, with every need met, every hour of every day.

Over and above this Ark was *a space* bordered by two Cherubims facing each other and with their wings spread in an arc, thus creating the space. Out from this space, (for there was nothing to see with the naked eye) was the *Mercy seat* and bursting forth from this Mercy Seat was the blazing and brilliant Shekinah Glory of God.

This is a name which describes God with a feminine gender, telling us that the *heart of God is Mercy* and that Mercy is the Motherhood of God.

Man has seen God as judgmental, demanding justice through exacting suffering. Man has altogether missed the true nature of God. For deep in the soul and core of the Source of all LIFE is a soft, but exceedingly powerful, feminine heart of pure Mercy. It is the most powerful force in God and the true and living way by which man is viewed.

Mercy is the ability to see the object of its love in the light of only perfection, innocence, and radiant beauty. Thereby causing this only to appear!

This is the mystery unveiled. God sees us in our true state of being, no matter how we choose to view ourselves. And this true image held in this pure heart of love is what corrects whatever seems to appear that needs correction! Therefore to stand before this Mercy Seat is to find true and permanent healing and restoration.

Now understand this: no man could enter this understanding, nor this experience, of God's true nature until the veil was torn open at the conclusion of the final Atonement Sacrifice. Why? Not because God intended this to be, but because the dark spirit of condemnation, separation and expectation of punishment which ruled the hearts of men could not grasp Mercy! And still doesn't. Man looked for punishment as a consequence for his sense of separation from God, his failure, his judgment of himself. Even though Mercy was all about him he could not grasp it. Until the Atonement Sacrifice ripped through the whole scenario and abolished any *sense* of separation, sin, punishment, disease, death. Now man is free from this belief...free from these experiences... and able to comprehend and embrace Mercy.

At least this is what is available. However, every time I speak of this and it falls on the ears of hard line religion I get a call or a letter, screaming and scathing, about the "justice of God" and how necessary it is for man to suffer for his offenses.

When will man realize that the justice of God *is*

the Mercy of God and that only "by *Mercy and truth* can iniquity ever be purged?"[11]

But to you who embrace this understanding...now you are free from this bondage. Now you are free to be bathed in the Light and Glory of Mercy. Now you can walk with your head held high and a joy in your step for you are free. No sense of dread. Nothing to block or stop you from accepting the Mercy of God and the grace to see it all appear for you. "Now we can come *boldly* to the throne of grace and receive grace and Mercy in time of need."[12] Oh the wonder of it all! That man would know, would understand, what is available to us all!

The indescribable Love that holds out its hand and opens its heart to us all. The Mercy that sees us and knows us all as pure, clean, whole, innocent, blameless. That welcomes us right now and forever into its Presence to bath in its Love and receive the grace we need for every situation.

"Come boldly to the throne of Mercy and receive, receive, receive."

It was this realization and this specific scripture that I held in my heart two years ago when I met a family that certainly needed Grace and Mercy.

One day, unannounced, they came bursting through the doors of the clinic carrying an infant girl crying "Please help my daughter. She is dying." Mother, father, grandparents, aunts, uncles, sister...the whole lot of them. And dying was exactly what was happening.

Her name was Casey. She was just under two years old. She was jaundiced, her belly was huge, and her eyes were sunken with black circles beneath them. She was bald from chemotherapy. They said she had liver cancer and was sent home from the hospital that very day... to die at home.

Little Casey whimpered and whimpered, too weak to cry. But the crying was there. She couldn't eat or drink because her belly was too swollen, both from liver disease and from months of chemotherapy causing a severely impacted colon. So we spent hours cleaning out her colon, opening it up so she could drink fluids at least. It took two days to get that impaction opened but we finally did. Soon she was drinking water and goat's milk and eating soft fruits. The whimpering slowed down some in intensity but still it continued. To say she was heavy on my heart is an understatement. I thought of nothing else.

In the middle of the night, probably two days after I met her, I was awakened by these two statements. One was, "They think they caused this." I knew immediately God was speaking about the parents of this child. The next word that followed was, "Ask them why they think she is sick."

This was not something I would normally do, but of course in this case I did, considering what I just heard. The next morning when they wheeled her buggy into the clinic, I took them aside in another room and sat down with them. I asked them as gently as I possibly could, "Do you have any idea why your baby might be sick?" Immediately they both began to cry and wail out loud. Their words were inaudible at first but soon it was clear they were saying, "You don't know how bad we have been!" Over and over they cried out those words and I was stunned into silence.

My mind flew back to that panel discussion I had just watched only days before. My heart was raw with the words of condemnation and human responsibility for failure that those men announced. Here were living proof and obvious consequences of such malicious doctrine. Here was the scripture fulfilled right before my eyes, "The strength of sin and disease is condemnation."[13]

Finally I gained enough composure to say these words, from deep in my soul. "No. You are right. I do not know how bad you have been." They became suddenly very quiet. "But I do know how good God is and that is the only factor that is present here. The goodness of God that swallows up any sense of "badness" you may have done."

The quietness continued…a strange stillness. Never in their lives had they heard such words of hope and Mercy. They were face to face with the truth of God, the Mercy of Infinite Love, for the first time in their lives. I asked them to stay for a meeting we were having that night that would help them to understand the words they just heard. They agreed.

I sure do love the Love of God! That night everyone gathered around those two parents. They knew nothing about what the child was suffering from. They knew nothing about the condemnation that the parents were feeling. But they responded to the Love that was in their hearts and they supported those two all evening. They touched them, held their hands, placed their arms around their shoulders. It was electrifying and it made me cry.

The mom and dad cried too. They were *receiving* Mercy and grace and forgiveness through the Love of those people. I could feel it. We were bathing in the Mercy of God, which was the subject of the talk that evening.

That night, deep in the wee hours of the morning, I took that little baby in my arms and carried her into the Holy of Holies and stood before the Mercy Seat. I never said a word. I stood in the Presence of such intense Glory, such as I had never felt before in my life. The Light was brilliant and warm and encompassing. The Love was palpable. We were immersed in something that could never be described. This whole experience lasted for what seemed to be hours. And finally I fell asleep.

The next day I placed my hand over her liver, as was customary for me to do, and for the first time it was small and soft, the way a liver should feel. She was smiling. Her color was normal, her eyes were clear. The dark circles had vanished. We knew she was healed. And she was!

She ate and ate. She was quiet but contented.

Two days later, at her doctor's visit, they said her healing was astounding, amazing. The liver enzymes in the blood studies were normal. The doctors lined up to feel her liver and just look at her.

To say that we were ecstatic with joy, really wild with excitement, would be understated. I have experienced thousands of healings in the span of my lifetime with patients, friends, family, people I knew and those I did not. But never have I been more immersed in joy. The parents simply cried with joy but were wordless, really kind of in shock, trying to comprehend what had just happened.

But on the evening of the fifth day of the healing they received a visit from their clergy. He was not happy with what he saw. He told them that they had lived a life of hell and needed to be punished for this. He felt that the punishment and "justice of God" had not been met! He reminded them of their offenses and the consequences of their sins. He poisoned their minds with his malignant doctrines until they sunk right back into the hell hole where we found them. The next day little Casey went to sleep and never woke up.

Stunned, horrified and paralyzed into silence, I attended her funeral. The same clergy stood in front of us all and said these words, "We don't know why these things happen." Then he looked at the parents and said, "Or do we?"

It took two people to hold me in my seat. I was screaming inside.

Sadly we never saw them again.

The obvious contrast between the Mercy that is God and the doctrines of men, is only too apparent. The obvious contrast between the mind of God and the minds of unenlightened men is also apparent. The contrast between life lived under the spirit of condemnation and life lived under the Spirit of Life is astonishing. "For the law of the Spirit of Life has made me free from the law of sin and death."[14]

And it is ours for the choosing.

We should not wait another minute to enter the Presence of Mercy right now, for whatever we need. Do not wait to "do it right." Do not wait to make the right prayer. Do not wait to feel worthy. Do not wait to qualify for this. There is no qualification. Just choose.

CHAPTER FIVE

THE NEW HEAVEN
AND THE NEW EARTH

A CHANGE IN CONSCIOUSNESS

Remember the words of the New Covenant, secured for us by the Atonement sacrifice. "A new heart will I give you, a new Spirit put within you. I will take away your stony heart. By my heart and Spirit now as your possession, you shall walk in my ways. (Grace) I will call you my people and I will be your God. There will be no remembrance of transgressions or offense, nothing to pay back or to suffer for. And in this place all shall know me from the least to the greatest."[1]

The Kingdom of God is a place in consciousness where we live *by the Spirit of Life within us.* Because we are filled with this Spirit *we will automatically live out from it.* Religion mostly teaches men to live the supernatural life by their own efforts. But here we know that we possess a Spirit and a Life that will *live out its own nature* through us with no effort at all.

For instance, if I am enraged by someone's actions, yet I am instructed to "go the second mile, to bless those who persecute, to turn the other cheek"[2]... I find it almost impossible to do this. Even if I could, it would not be spontaneous but an effort. But if I am filled with the Spirit of God, if God is my entire conscious life, then I would *naturally* respond to that in my heart and it would now be my *nature* to go the second mile.

Even though man has read the words of Matthew (chapter 5) for two thousand years, we have never been able to meet those requirements fully because we have attempted to do this by our own efforts. Those words describe the heart of one who lives in the Kingdom of God and therefore can only be lived by the Spirit of God. Again we turn to Divine Source to live it for us, through us, as us.

This is a choice. *And every choice we make has the consequence of the very choice itself.* We choose... and grace does the work. We choose and grace causes the heart and soul of God to appear for every situation. Gone are the days of religious effort and subsequent failure. This can only be lived by the Spirit of God alone.

In Isaiah, chapter 58, we read these words: "If you will honor the Lord by keeping holy the Sabbath, by not doing thy own works, not going thy own way or even speaking thy own words..."[3] This is the description of one who is fully trusting in the activity of grace to live this life. This is also one who realizes that we are here to do the will of God because we belong to him who sent us here. We have come to fulfill a purpose greater than our own! The whole chapter is so powerful. It might be good here to stop and read it.

The Kingdom of God is primarily governed by Mercy. Remember that it is the Mercy of God that heals, never punishment or inflicting suffering. It is this Spirit that we now possess. Therefore it is natural for us to rise up in forgiveness and Mercy when confronted by an offense. The goal is never to *be right* but always to heal. If I, by turning the other cheek, (think differently, turn from the natural human response) can release the Mercy and Love the offender needs, then it is my joy to do so.

God does not react to offenses. "Blessed is the man who knows the law of Love, nothing shall in any way offend him."[4] The one who bears the Spirit of Christ will also not react. In the nature of man this is impossible to do, but in the nature of Mercy it is the natural way to respond.

If there is only one truth and understanding you glean from this work, let it be the complete acceptance of this ONE TRUTH...God does not react to us, for good or evil. God just IS what he is. We either accept it for our good or reject it because we think we have not earned it...and we think we must earn it.

A little girl, not more than 9 years old, sat in my office a few days ago and told me that she had a lot of "tummy aches." She was rubbing her tummy while she spoke. "I know God gives me these tummy aches when I don't read my Bible enough." This is just the beginning of such violent, pernicious and malignant beliefs about the workings of God. The beginning of living by condemnation, blame and guilt. The creation of a god who does not exist.

Eating from the tree of the knowledge of good and evil[5] is seeing yourself and others as capable of both good and evil, as containing within one's self both consciousnesses. Conversely, eating from the tree of Life is seeing yourself and others as possessing the one and only consciousness, the Infinite Mind of God which always causes Life in all of its goodness to appear.

Obviously, if we *look to what is humanly appearing as the truth* we will never be able to break away from eating of the tree of good and evil...and so we continue to suffer and die.

Again this is a choice, and a very critical one at that! "While we look not at those things which are seen, but at that which is unseen."[6]

All along we have been told, and believed, that we really do possess the capacity for both good and evil. By starting from this ideology we are then to *gain* the Mind of God by following the words and works of Jesus, for he was sent to teach us the way of holiness.

But for over two thousand years man has tried and failed. We still "bite and devour one another."[7] We still suffer strife and divisions. We still war and see separateness between men and nations. We still suffer the belief that disease can rule over us and we are nothing more than victims of its madness.

We are trying to reach a level of life *without the burden of the sin consciousness* through many religious rituals, all bespeaking human effort. All destined to fail.

But one cannot, with a mind that embraces duality, ever bring out a mind of pure oneness! We must first begin with the understanding and sure conviction that there is only One Mind and, in spite of generations of man believing in two minds and seeing the results of what he has chosen to believe, there has only been One Mind all along. The other is a projection of a belief and no more. This results in insanity, which is a good description of the world thought. "For there is one Spirit and that results in One Body, which is The Christ, the fullness of him which fills all."[8]

People are always referring to their "ego" or "selfhood" as a conflicting entity that they must overcome. Not at all! The only thing to overcome is a *belief* that you could possibly possess something that God did not create. If we believe we actually possess two minds, we will continue to try to win over the one by building up the other. This is religion. And it has and will continue to fail.

We must begin with the knowledge that all along there has only been One Mind, one Heart, one Spirit, one Life and we have been the visible manifestations of that only. No matter what tries to appear, we must stand our ground. Do not get into trying to heal what has appeared. Hold to the basic fact that nothing has any legitimate right to appear for there is no other Presence or Power that exists, except as a projection of this idea. It is but a vapor, a fog. You can right now get up and walk right through that into the sunlight of truth and victory.

I choose to believe that Infinite Love appeared as Jesus. I choose to believe that the words he spoke to us were indeed the Wisdom of God for us. I choose to believe that the miracles he did were to prove that the Kingdom truly is here now and these works are easily available for each one to do...if we choose.

I choose to know that he came to prove that there is only One Mind, one Life, one Being and *we all* live out from that. There is no other way to live the spiritual life successfully. There is no other way to live in victory, in Love (in him) and in the goodness of Life. There is no other way to live out from under the influence of the sin consciousness.

When Jesus did away with the sin consciousness, he did away with the belief of it, for it never was a reality. (Again read the 8th, 9th and 10th chapters of Hebrews) If there is no sin consciousness, what then are we still struggling with and why?

I choose to believe that the purpose for the crucifixion was to remove from us the entire sin consciousness with all of its resultant consequences. I choose to believe that the sin consciousness includes the entire sense of separation from who we really are. That includes seeing myself, or you, as less than "The fullness of him that fills all and in all."[9] "For we are his masterpiece, created in perfection."[10]

So instead of trying to *gain* this state of wonder and goodness...it is left to us to simply accept it now...no matter what is appearing to us.

Only receive! Spread your arms wide open before the goodness and blazing glory of Divine Love and Mercy and receive, receive, receive. Open your heart before him and let the flow of this One Life be realized as *your Life*. This is the only valid meditation which is eternally productive. Not using meditation to visualize what you want to happen, but accepting the whole of the Mind and Spirit of the One Life as your essence and as your Being. This is receiving the "new heart and new spirit"[11] spoken to us as the fulfillment of the New Covenant. Soon everything will appear to you new and clean and wonderful, for he is wonderful. "Behold, I make all things new."[12]

This is the "new heaven and new earth."[13]

I cannot begin a prayer believing that what I am seeing is real if I am seeing anything less than the fullness of God in the entire Christ body. I must begin my prayer by looking at the Nature of God which never changes...no matter what is seen. *It is that which always produces the healing.*

Many years ago I was looking at a LIFE magazine. It was a special edition to commemorate the past fifty years. The cover was a collage of pictures which captured the major events. I sat and looked at them trying to see how many I could identify. I saw the famous picture of the little girl running naked, screaming in pain from the severe burns she received by the napalm bombing in Saigon. I saw Jackie Kennedy in the blood soaked, pink suit with Lyndon Johnson taking the oath of office next to her. I saw the three exhaust trails of smoke as the Challenger blew up. On and on it went. Suddenly my eye caught a picture of a very thin, black boy about 9 years old, sitting naked on a rock. He was so emaciated. He looked to be almost his birth weight, and I knew it was speaking of the (then) present famine in Ethiopia. My heart wrenched within me and I jumped up and began to pray.

But where to begin? I thought about praying for the food that we sent to get through the various political obstructions. I thought of several things, my heart running ahead of my mind. But then I stopped. I asked God how to pray. And this is what I heard:

"Do you think I would, or could, abandon my beloved children like this? Do I not 'Open my hand and satisfy the desire of every living thing?'[14] Do they need to qualify for my care? Does anyone need to qualify for my love? Do not start with a lie about me simply because of what your eyes see. Declare the truth. Choose the truth. Hold the truth in your heart only, and the picture will be corrected before the eyes of men."

With that I began to declare the goodness of God as the Father, Provider and Source of every living thing. I knew that he is the Essence and Life of every man, woman and child. I knew he held his creation intact, and in harmony and peace. No matter what man was seeing, it was merely a projection, an image out from beliefs of good and evil. No matter what, God had never changed, therefore the truth had never changed. I spoke of this for several minutes, maybe an hour. It all appeared so clear to me that *the picture* was reduced to the insanity that it always is.

Within days it was announced that the famine was lifted.

We cannot start with the false picture and then ask God to fix what he never could allow to start with. If the picture is true about God then it is true. But if the picture is not true about the nature of God, then it is false. A result of man's projection of good and evil. Something simply appearing on the canvas of the mind.

"Whatsoever God has made shall be forever. Nothing can be added to it nor can anything be taken from it. And God does this that men should stand in awe of him forever."[15]

When you are praying for a relationship that appears fractured, you must forget the right and wrongs. You must forget who did what and who didn't. Is God fractured? Can God be divided? Is God the Life of every living thing? Is God the Life of the people involved? Is there One Life? Do you choose to eat of the tree of One Life or to remain judging right and wrong? Your choice will determine the outcome. Always look to the nature of God in every situation. That only will tell you what to choose, what to hold in your heart.

When facing a disease of mind or body ask yourself: Can God fall into disrepair? Is God the Creator of man? Of the body of man? Do we look to the Source of the life of the body to tell us how the body is, or do we look to the tests and beliefs of man? Do we first believe the tests, the appearances, and then ask God to fix it? Does God see the works of his hands falling apart? "All the works of his hands are perfect."[16] Are we the works of his hands?

When facing betrayal, or any obtrusive behavior, stop and question yourself again. Has the sin consciousness really been removed from the hearts of men? Do we wait to see it before we believe it? Or do we choose this day to know that every man, woman and child is altogether innocent, faultless, blameless, holy and Divine? Was the sacrifice of Jesus enough? When he said, "It is finished,"[17] do we choose to believe this?

The word "radical" means to get to the root of something...and we must be very radical to see this Kingdom of God everywhere we look.

This is how Jesus healed. He saw what never changes. He refused to believe what his eyes saw, but *chose to see with his heart instead*. He chose to be *faithful to the truth of God and never allow the pictures, images of men, to dictate his beliefs*. He lived by <u>the standard of the Nature of God</u>, measuring everything that appeared against that immutable reality. He chose Life in every instance. And so must we.

He said that it was by the grace and Spirit of God that he was able to do the works that he did and it is by the very same Spirit and grace that we do the works as well. He knew that the power rested in his *choice of belief*... "As you have believed, so it shall be done."[18]

The sin consciousness with all its *mortal identity* is gone, buried. And we live by choice, in the Kingdom of perpetual goodness and Love. Our identity now must be as the Christ of God (*in him*), come to be his Light to all darkness that appears along our way.[19]

"For this mortal must put on immortality and this corruptible must put on incorruption."[20]

Today this scripture is fulfilled. This is how it is done.

For centuries we have been told that we needed to

gain this by dying, by suffering, by blood, sweat and tears. In the absence of the mortal identity, in the absence of the sin consciousness this is fulfilled. Choose. Make the choice with your words. Make the choice in your heart. Grace will cause the fulfillment to appear.

CHAPTER SIX

SOURCE OR SELF-RELIANCE

Now that we have accepted Heaven as our present home, how do we live?

The first principle, and maybe the most important is this, we look to the Source of all Life to be the Source of our every need. We realize it is ever flowing to us and through us. We fully accept that it is immediately and abundantly available, and we live in appreciation for it.

God reveals the Glory of his Nature through your consciousness. He communicates with you through your consciousness.

That sense of "awareness of you being you" that we all feel now and again, individual and separate from all other manifestations of Creation, is God making his Presence known, in you...as you.

God is the great I Am. When you are the most cognizant of yourself as "I" you are experiencing the "Oneness" of you and your Creator, the Source and Essence of your Life.

God is Love and God is the only Creator. *Everything that appears is really Infinite Love appearing* as that object, that person, that opportunity, that "open door" you are looking at. We must learn to "see God" instead of simply seeing things, or people.

We must come quickly to the point of seeing *everything* as Infinite Love appearing for our good. When you awake in the early morning and hear the birds singing, you must know that Love, Itself, is welcoming you to another day.

When you feel the wind blowing against your face, you must be acutely aware of the Presence of God speaking softly to you.

Every tree is Love shading you from the heat of the sun or offering food and nourishment.

Every flower declares to you the many faces of the beauty and Glory of God.

All things are for you.

When you realize every person you are in contact with is Love standing before you, that realization will touch their hearts and open each one for whatever healing or blessing they need.

Your children will respond to your new awareness of them as actually being Love incarnate. Your spouse, your friends, your co-workers, everyone you happen upon each day will feel an uncanny, but undeniable connection with God when they are in your presence.

"For you shall see him as he truly is."[1]

The Spirit of God in you will bear witness to the Spirit of God in them and there will be a palpable unity. It will awaken the sleeping Christ within them and they will feel alive, whole and complete. Wonderful things will appear in their lives.

My five year old granddaughter entered kindergarten still not knowing her letters. She was confused and seemed uninterested in learning. Her attention span concerning all this was somewhere around zero. Give her a baby doll to care for and she could do that by the hours!

In kindergarten they score the children from zero to five based on their ability to know their letters and to read words. To advance to first grade they need to be at a five or more. In spite of individual tutoring, by Christmas she was still at zero.

This is how I prayed...

I am extremely aware of her as Infinite Love appearing for our joy. I see Love flowing through her and as her, quite easily. Now, some of the qualities of God are knowledge, intelligence, and understanding. This is the One, Eternal, Divine Mind and *she cannot be separated from that manifestation and activity.*

I saw in my mind a "space" in her that needed to be realized as containing this quality of God.

So, knowing that God "knows no vacuum," I invited this...I chose this...to fill that space. Actually I chose for us all to become aware that it always had, and will continue to, fill that space!

As her mom and dad, teachers and tutors worked with her, encouraging and supporting her efforts, as my daughter's prayers for her little girl continued...she suddenly began to read. In six weeks she had advanced from zero to five and now nothing could stop her.

"Behold I have set before you an open door that no man can shut."[2]

This is how God is realized in the consciousness of anyone when there seems to be a need or a lack.

If I had prayed for God to fix her I would have been starting with the belief that something is wrong with her. This would be contrary to the reality that she is, even now and always, "complete in him."[3] This would be a belief that she was separate from all the fullness of God. "Of his fullness have we all received."[4] This would leave me "hoping" that God would do what I needed him to do. But God is not "doing." God is *Being*.

I cannot begin a prayer with all that erroneous belief going on. I cannot begin a prayer denying so much of the truth and then hope to see a "miracle."

We are instructed by Jesus to "pray believing that YOU HAVE ALREADY RECEIVED and you shall receive."[5]

How do we do that? By realizing that there is no separation. There is no God outside of you who you hope will fix you. There is no separation for we are *In him*, now and always.

Once you establish this in your mind, you know you already have all of him and "all that I have is yours."[6] It is then just a matter of holding it in your consciousness, or in your heart if you prefer, of you agreeing with the absolute truth of God and man. This is your prayer, your confidence. "We are his temple, the *fullness* of him that fills all and in all."[7] "We are now, and always have been, complete in him."[8]

We have only two choices as I see it. We can look to the Source for our Wisdom, our understanding, our needs, our purpose, our path, or we can look to ourselves or to another "arm of flesh."[9] "Go not down to Egypt to trust in the horses and chariots of Egypt. For they are flesh and not my Spirit."[10]

It might seem easier to look to man. It might seem more convenient and quicker, but the way is precarious, not well defined and a roll of the dice. One way is sure, the other is scary, unsure.

Isaiah 43:12 says, "I have declared and I have saved you from harm when *there was no strange god among you.*" What is a strange god? Anything we put our trust in that is not drawing from the heart of God.

So we read in the second commandment given to Moses, "Thou shall not have strange gods among you."[11]

Why? Because it will destroy us. The wisdom of man is no wisdom at all. It will promise deliverance, but it will ultimately fail us.

There are four books of the Old Testament that talk about the years and generations when kings ruled the children of Israel.[12] As each king is introduced to us, it is stated whether he was a "good" king or an "evil" king. And the deciding factor in every case was not if he was without faults, was not that he never fell flat on his face, but only if he "sought the Lord all the days of his life, or if he instead sought strange gods."[13] This was called "worshipping in the groves and high places."[14] It was also referred to as "playing the harlot with every stranger under every green tree."[15] The green tree was the promise of life as we turn from the Wisdom of God to the ways of men.

Simply put, a strange god is anything we put our trust in, our hope in, other than God, the Source of it all.

When we determine to let go of human props, which are rubber crutches at best, and turn to Divine Wisdom with our whole hearts as our only Source of supply, we really get to know him in a way most people do not. We find such faithfulness and devotion. We find that he really "will never leave you or forsake you."[16] We find healings and deliverances that we could only dream of. We find a strong sense of security in an otherwise insecure world. We feel loved and cherished. People may withhold their love at times, but we never feel a lack of Love.

"Look unto me all ye ends of the earth and be ye saved from all harm...for I am God and there is none else."[17]

Time and again we are warned to look only to Source for our help.

Why is this so important to God? Because he loves us. Because he wants to see us walk in safety and security. Because he wants us to experience every good and wonderful thing. Because he wants a living, breathing, vibrant relationship with us every minute of every day.

As we lean to man and the myriads of ways and means of help offered, we realize deep within us that it is a roll of the dice. It may help, but it may not help at all. It may make things worse. It may leave us in worse shape than before. So we feel fear, insecure within our hearts. We wish we knew the future so we could make better decisions...but we can't. The fear keeps us tense, unsure, and in this state we cannot heal anything or be healed.

Only Divine Mind knows the future...and we know him. So as we yield to his Wisdom we feel peaceful and well loved. In this condition we will always heal.

But the ability to heal cannot take place in a state of paralyzing fear.

Jesus often healed people on the Sabbath day. This infuriated the religious leaders of his day. They were so legalistic and rigid, because they did not possess the Spirit or understanding of the words of the law. They taught fear and they lived fear. One day I realized why he did that.

The word Sabbath means "rest." We are instructed to "enter into the rest of God."[18] Be peaceful, be confident in Love's love for you. Trust the faithfulness of God. Learn to hear his Voice and understand his directions. Ask him to teach you how to do this. He will. It is in this peaceful state of quietness that our bodies and hearts are healed.

Many healings that I have seen have happened when the person is sleeping at night, or even in a coma! They have "ceased from their own works"[19] and are in a state of rest.

The tension we live in on a daily basis is not conducive to health or wholeness. This tension is a result of feeling personally responsible for our lives. One day God spoke to me that I was living in a "sense of urgency."

I was always going headlong into whatever was going on. I never casually did anything. I drove my car like my life depended on getting wherever I was going. Even if I wasn't in a hurry to get there, I drove like I was.

I heard what he said, but I really didn't know how to correct it. *Then I knew that I wasn't to correct it at all but simply to choose* to live in more quietness and confidence, peace and "rest." The choice I made that day was soon to change my life. I have never before lived in such a state of quiet confidence... a calmness that I have enjoyed since I made that choice.

When we "make a choice" we release the choice to the grace of God. That grace will carry the choice to fulfillment every time. But if we make a choice, then immediately jump up and begin to try to fulfill it ourselves we block the grace of God by all our efforts and striving and the choice remains dormant. The reason we jump up and try to do something is because we don't trust that grace will do it.

So many times I have heard it said, "I have made the choice, but nothing is happening. I must be doing something wrong." It is the insistence of thinking that you must still *do something* that is blocking your ability to see that something actually already IS going on.

This lack of trust is the reason for self-reliance...the enemy of trust. The enemy of grace. The enemy of success in living out from our home...heaven.

The first and foremost reason we don't trust is because we really don't know the true nature of God. And because we have been poisoned by the many aberrant ideologies repeated endlessly about God. It will take God himself to reach our hearts with his true Love and nature. "Acquaint yourself with him and be at peace."[20] "To know God aright is Life Eternal."[21]

This is one desire you can bet that God will fill as soon as you ask...as soon as you choose.

Above all else God is Love. The very name *God* comes from the Saxon word for good. Unlike what we have been told, God is only and always good. No matter anything about us, any way we have failed, any way we have lived...God is always good. When we don't see that it is because we don't open our hearts to receive it. "The rain falls on the just and unjust alike."[22] The Love that God is, is impartial...it does not "give" if you are good and "deny" if you are not so good. "The sun shines on the evil and unthankful as well."

It can only respond to its own nature. "It cannot deny itself."[23]

Probably the greatest lesson we can learn is that truth. As humans we respond to others. We open our hearts to love if we are loved. We give if someone gives to us. We are kind if we receive kindness. But not so with Divine Love. It is Love. It cannot be other than what it is. Love is Love no matter what. If we open our hearts to know this and choose to receive it, we certainly will.

The second reason we don't trust is a direct result of the idea that we are mortals, born of a man and woman and therefore subject to failure and defeat. As the previous chapters declare, that opens us up to the expectation of punishment for failure. If we really believe that, we could never fully trust anything, always waiting for the deserved pain to begin.

Very early on while I was reading the gospel of John, I noticed that Jesus often referred to himself as one who was *sent*. Not born, but sent. This idea of being sent really went deep into my soul. "As my father sent me so send I you."[24]

I quickly circled in red ink every time he said the word "sent." It appeared so often in that book that I knew it was pivotal. I also knew it was talking about me, about you, about us all. We must come to the realization that we are spiritual beings, in spite of how we have defined ourselves in the past. We have been alive in him forever. We will always be alive in him.

We must also come to know that we are purposeful. There is a definite reason that we have been sent... and God has made himself responsible for the total out-working of that purpose.

Job declared, "He will fulfill the reason for which I have been sent."[25]

The full realization of these two points will cause us to feel significant, cherished and watched over with great care. We will know we belong to him who sent us here. We will know that he will cover us from any harm and we are eternally safe in his care. We will stop trying to gain something. Stop trying to achieve spiritual success. Stop trying to please God, for God is so pleased with us already. If we only knew this we would never believe that we live under the *law of chance*. That anything could happen to us at any time over which we would have no recourse. We would live safely, securely and peacefully under the *law of continual Love and care*. No chance here. No fear here.

We will laugh at self reliance. We will see it as the empty prop that it really is. We will realize that it has its root in the pride of life as well as the fear of life. We will run to Divine Love and Wisdom for our answers, our direction. Finally we will see the fulfillment of this Christ Life in and through us as we allow the Source of it all to flow and BE.

For the clarity of understanding, the Old Testament is an account of man deep in the grips of self reliance. Depending upon his own abilities to bring about righteousness before God and subsequently failing in his efforts. Believing that he will be blessed by these efforts and also believing he must be the one to create righteousness, he continued even after failure was evident.

The New Testament is the account of man who finally realized that righteousness was a part of his inherent nature as one born of God... and grace, the activity of the Spirit of God, would bring it forth in his life. The more we understand and depend upon grace, the quicker we will see the goodness of a life of righteousness.

Biblically we are told again and again to follow the Spirit in this earth walk. To look only to the Divine Source for all our needs and for all direction. To cease from human struggle.

King Saul lost the kingdom because he refused to look to Source for direction. When the going got tough, he ran ahead of God and did it his own way. He lacked discipline and trust. The daughters of Lot,[26] when they looked at their circumstances and determined that there would be no husbands for them, therefore they would never have children, manipulated their father, got him drunk, and had sexual relations with him. Both daughters became pregnant. The name of the first son born was Moab. His name meant "trusting in your own efforts." The second son born was called Amman, meaning "trusting in your treasures, your position, your powers." Both of these sons grew to become nations unto themselves. They were constantly at war with the children of Israel throughout their wilderness journey. This tells us that we will come up against this temptation often in our lives, to trust in our own efforts and our own accomplishments, but we are to be diligent and watchful to remember that no situation is outside of the control of the Divine Intelligence who watches over us. He only is the Source of our life.

Abraham was told by God that he would bear a son that would be the Father of all nations.[27] He believed God, but as the years went on and he and Sarah still had not conceived a son, their faith began to wax and wane. Thirteen years had passed. At this point Sarah decided to fix this herself. She gave her servant Hagar to Abraham to have a son with her. And so they did and Ishmael was born. But God said to Abraham that this was not the promised son. For centuries, as it still is today, there has been war between the son they brought forth that day and the promised son. Spiritually this is speaking of the internal conflict we create when we "run ahead of God" in any area of our lives.

Twelve years after Ishmael was born, (twenty five years after the promise was given) when Sarah was 99 years old and Abraham was 100 years old, they gave birth to Isaac, the promised son.[28]

I have personally "given birth" to so many "Ishmaels" in my life from "running ahead of God"... because I began to faint when the days and weeks turned into months and years. So much unnecessary pain and confusion. Finally we do learn though. Some quicker than others. He is faithful to his word but the only way we will see this is when we "cease from our own works"[29] and choose to trust.

There are many stories and many words of Jesus that assure us of the provision of God in financial needs. We must remember that we do not live by what we make in a job, but we live out from the endless resources of "he who made it all."[30] Even when the picture looks impossible, if we are faithful to look to Source, we will find the resources we need. We must see our work as an opportunity to love and support others in their journey towards awakening. As we are faithful to do this, we find the goodness of God far surpasses whatever the monetary supply of the job. We had a saying in Bible College, "You can't out-give God giving." No matter how much you give, God will always give more to you. "Whatsoever thy hand finds to do, do it with all your heart as unto the Lord and not to man."[31] Everything we do must be for the Glory of God and not for our own gain--not even our "jobs." God supplies...we just give.

When I began the clinic in 1975 I felt that I was never to advertise for clients. I reasoned that if I was directed by Divine Guidance to do this, he would bring those who could benefit from our work to us. That would increase my confidence that he also would heal them that he sent. Many times I was approached to advertise but I always said no. Without a word about what I was doing, from the beginning we were thronged by folks looking for help and feeling "directed" to come to us, as it still is today.

Even in praying for someone needing help, I never presume to know what or how to pray. I always begin by turning to the Wisdom of God for direction. Once I feel a direction I will pray. Again this increases confidence that they will respond to the healing that is offered.

You are here for a specific purpose. It is first to know God. It is then to respond to a vital relationship with him. It is also for a specific work that is held in the heart of Love. You cannot know this unless you first choose to allow him to direct your steps towards that path. To live in this Kingdom of God, this reign of Love and harmony, is to know the "joy of purpose" in your life.

I remember meeting a man who, as a child, was held back in school several times because he could not grasp the lessons being taught. No matter how many tutors he had, he yet remained in a darkened understanding. His mother prayed for direction and received the instruction to have him memorize the book of Proverbs during a summer vacation. Together they worked on this everyday and by the end of the summer months his mind had opened and he was able to not only catch up with the others his age, but he surpassed them altogether. Eventually he had two PhDs and a thriving worldwide ministry.

I often tell the story of a young woman in her early twenties who followed her heart and moved to a religious farm in Alaska to learn and serve her God. After a few years she became restless and desired to marry and have children. But the farm was small and the available men were few. She was a beautiful girl but was almost 6 feet tall and wanted to marry a man taller than herself. There was no one who fit the requirements, so she announced to the pastor that she was going back to the "lower states." He spoke to her about trusting the resources of Infinite Love even when the picture looks impossible. In his words, "God could drop a man out of the sky for you!" She decided to pray and wait for the fulfillment of her desire.

Four months later a group of young men were participating in "wilderness rescue skills" training and the last thing required was to parachute out of a small plane. The wind was blowing and the instructor, the last to jump, was blown off direction and landed right in the middle of their camp. He was 6'6" tall and unmarried. A year later she was married and two years later began her family. "No good thing will I withhold from them that seek me."[32] "I have freely given you all things."[33]

Love, by its very nature cannot withhold.

After many years occupying three buildings in downtown San Antonio, the clinic received a gift of land out in beautiful Boerne, Texas. We moved and placed the three buildings for sale. Surprisingly they did not sell. The first one we practically gave away, which was grievous to me. Another had many people looking at it and I was confident would soon sell. But the third and largest one was chopped up with too many small rooms and I thought that one probably would be the last to go. My realtor was sometimes as frustrated as I was. We all prayed and we all believed, but nothing was happening. I asked God why?

One day, after returning from a trip, I called her to tease her and I asked, "Did you sell the buildings while I was gone?" She said, "No, but I did have a dream about it." She dreamed that I was showing her this large building for the first time and asking her to sell it for me. But it was a palace, enormous and radiant in its beauty. It was all in marble, granite and gold and it shone as the mid-day sun. She kept exclaiming, "Oh, Michele, it is so beautiful. You never told me how beautiful it was."

After we hung up the phone I asked God what the dream meant and this was my answer, very clear! "You have never seen it as it truly is. You have minimized the beauty of it in your mind and therefore so it is in the minds of others. Choose to see it as I see all things. Choose to elevate its significance in your mind." And so I did.

I thought of the folks we are caring for at the clinic. I thought that if they would choose to see the beauty, choose to realize the magnificence of their being they would allow that to appear. I thought of how "beat down" we allow ourselves to get and how insignificant we see ourselves and others. I thought of the contrast between what we feel about ourselves and what God sees us to be. I prayed for our hearts to open to this. I prayed that we would all receive this true and eternal image of how things really are. Oh, how our expectations would increase and our lives would so reflect this!

God is the Source of our thoughts, images and expectations, if only we would allow him to be!

CHAPTER SEVEN

NO JOURNEY

I feel that I cannot repeat this enough, for this is the one stumbling block to living the Christ life and fulfillment of our purpose.

Given the acceptance of this Atonement and its life altering consequences, we can begin to see that this is not a result of anything we have done or need to do. We actually bring nothing to the table, so to speak. Any efforts of man to achieve, be holy, follow religion's many formulas and paths are simply by-passed as "much ado about not much." Any activity of man, by way of psychology or any other of the myriads of man-made remedies, are leaning to the "arm of flesh"[1] alone. Unless we are specifically led and instructed to use a particular method, this is an activity of grace from beginning to end. It is entirely a work of Mercy and Love, so great is Love's love for us all.

So why are we here? What is divine Wisdom's purpose for our being?

There is nothing we DO not Have!

Mortal thinking will see this experience we call *life* as a journey to gain something we don't have. Such as God's favor, heaven when we die, a specific healing or the like. There is no journey. There is nothing we don't have. We are from beginning to end the image of the Eternal Light of God. As we understand and accept God's provision for us to be able to climb out from under the rubble of the entire atmosphere of condemnation, we are able to finally realize a far greater purpose for us than self-preservation or self-achievement.

In the beginning the earth (human thinking) was without form and void (no understanding). There was confusion, chaos, no order, no form, just a void waiting to be filled with truth, with order, with form, with meaning, with purpose, with God.[2]

Darkness covered the face of the deep. And God said, "Let there be light."[3]

And you appeared.

Every time there is confusion, chaos, disorder, darkness...no matter how it presents itself (disease, despair, conflict, human hate, etc.)...it is a space that God, (Order, Substance, Truth, Being) must occupy. And this is where you come in. You appear as the Light to every darkness! You are the Light to every miserable, painful, confused situation that you face...otherwise you wouldn't be facing it.

When you know this and you BECOME the Light to it. And as it begins to be filled with Light, the darkness simply disappears. And you have fulfilled your purpose for ever being sent to it.

The world says this darkness "came upon you." No! You came upon it! You are the light. Every time you shine the Light of truth upon any darkness, that darkness becomes Light itself. That space is now occupied by Light and the Kingdom of God or Heaven is realized in that place. You fulfilled the purpose for appearing at that time in that place.

"Take dominion and subdue the fowls of the air (thoughts) and the fish of the sea (thoughts)."[4] Every dark situation begins with a thought, a belief, a misunderstanding of what truly is. By learning how to fill that space with truth, we bring Light to that darkness and we call that a healing.

That is why we are sent here. Not to gain heaven, for Jesus said that the Kingdom of God was already within you. Not to suffer to be purified of your many offenses and transgressions. For you are and always have been the "righteousness of God in Christ."[5] "He is made unto us wisdom, *righteousness*, redemption and sanctification."[6] "As he is in heaven, so are we in the earth."[7]

We are as we have been created and nothing can ever alter that. No matter how we have been taught to view our miserable lives, God's view of us has never changed. There is that within each one of us which has always known this, but it has been silenced by the loud shrieking of religion as it announces our unworthiness to be who we are.

God told us in the beginning not to enter into judgment of ourselves. Not to entertain the endless "inner critic" that "accuses us day and night before God."[8] He said "Do not eat of the tree of good and evil, for the day you do you shall surely die."[9] You shall die to who you are. You shall forget your true home, where you came from and why you were here.

When Adam (mortal identity) began to listen to the endless chatter of unending judgment against himself, he "hid himself"[10] from God for he felt ashamed. The word *ashamed* here means *to lack.* He felt a lack of his Light and Glory. How could he feel himself the Light and Glory of God while he listened about his perpetual state of unworthiness? He felt naked. Unclothed with Light and Glory. Unclothed with purity and righteousness. Unclothed with power and dominion. God said, "Who told you you were unclothed?"[11] God certainly didn't. God still doesn't.

If we continue to believe we are lost mortals, *on a journey* to achieve Heaven, but too unworthy to do so without suffering to purify us, we will continue to allow disease, pain, wars, divorce, loss and lack and limitation of every kind into our lives. *We will never challenge their right to overcome us. We will never feel the God-given authority to subdue them. We will continue on this endless journey to nowhere.*

We don't need more journeys. We need an *awakening* to what is here now, and always has been. We need to rise up in the magnitude of our Glory and be who we were sent here to be. He calls us a king, we need to act like a king. He calls us his beloved Son, we need to live like his beloved Son.

The idea of being on a journey makes us self absorbed. It is always about us. How far we think we have achieved. How far we think we need to go. How are we doing on the purification idea? We become a critic of not only our endless faults, but of how we are doing on this spiritual journey... to whatever. We see ourselves as a work in progress. In doing so we deny who we are.

We are not here for us. We are here for the sake of the Kingdom of God. We are here to see this realm of radiant beauty and order and harmony and peace established in and on and through this whole earth experience.

Jesus said that the Kingdom was here already and all we needed to do to experience this was to "repent."[12] The word repent means to think differently. This is what we are trying to do right now, we are CHOOSING to think differently. Every healing he did, every miracle he performed was to prove that the Kingdom is already here. He proved that Life had the power over death. He proved that the word of truth had the power over all disease, disorder, confusion. He proved that by "Mercy and truth iniquity is purged."[13] Not by suffering and pain and tragedy.

Another name for the Kingdom of God is the Christ consciousness. When we are filled with the reality of our Christ-consciousness it will create all the confidence we need to heal whatever appears in our path. But when we struggle about feeling full of fault and unworthy and "just wrong" we have no confidence and darkness overcomes us.

"No weapon formed against you can prosper."[14] When will that be true? So far every weapon formed against man has overcome him. This is because we have been taught to be the victim of whatever suffering is thrown at us. After all, we reason, we need it and it will be just the experience that will gain heaven for us. After we die. Maybe.

No wonder Jesus said of the religious voice, "You make the truth of God of *no effect* by your doctrines and traditions of thought."[15] "You close heaven to others and you yourself cannot enter in."[16] "You are the blind, leading the blind...both have fallen into the ditch."[17]

The key here is not human effort, not a journey to become worthy, or to learn truth. The key here is to *accept* what already is. Don't wait till you see something different. Don't wait until you, by your own assessment of yourself, have finally "arrived." Don't look to yourself at all. Look to God only. Look to the Atonement only. Look to Divine Love's assessment of you...made in his own image, perfect, whole, complete, incorruptible, uninterruptible, undefiled.

When we look to ourselves we will fail to be able to receive. But when we look to God, to his purpose and his grace, we will find it simple to open wide our hearts and receive all that he is and all that he declares us to be.

It is no different than when we are holding the truth for a healing. If we look to the patient, to the problem, to the symptoms, to the ugly human picture, we will never see what is behind the scene, the eternal and true. But when we, by choice, look beyond the hysteria and insanity presenting itself, and we never take our eyes off his infinite Glory and Mercy, the change appears in due time. People are always saying to me, "How can I see this person healed?" You can't. But you can and must look away from that disgraceful lie and look deep into the heart and Glory of God. For as God is, so is man in his sight. Forget man and all the confusion man has imagined, you can't make the lie become the truth. You must fill your mind and heart with the Glory of the true God and the human picture will be swallowed up in the Presence of his Glory.

Not only is our eternal purpose identified and fulfilled by grace, and not by any human effort, but so are the various and individual situations in each personal life made perfect by grace.

Yet so much that we have been taught has put the burden of responsibility for our lives upon us. From childhood to old age we feel our success depends on our ability to "do life right." It was thought to be irresponsible to expect God to do for us. How many times have we heard this insidious lie being repeated: "God helps those who help themselves." Nowhere is this found in any Sacred Scripture, anywhere. No! God helps those who put their trust in him. Period!

Our job is to choose Life, his eternal Life, for every situation. God then honors our choice and grace immediately begins to flow to correct, to create, to harmonize. "Behold, I have set before you life and death. Therefore choose life that you and your children may live."[18] Nowhere does it say that once we make this choice for Life, we then must begin to try to figure out how to create things differently. No! Grace does it for us.

I often hear folks say to me, "I have prayed and prayed, asked and chosen, but I must be missing something here because things just aren't changing." To say that you "must be missing something" says to me that you still think that there is something God is requiring you to do.

Actually he is. He wants you to stop thinking, reasoning and fretting and start praising and glorifying so that your heart may be open to receive. He requires you to trust the working out of every situation to him. Infinite Love is more than willing and more than capable.

Remember that "your life is not your own."[19] You belong to your Creator. This is really the only way you will ever have confidence and peace for every situation. Once the true nature of God is realized, down deep in your heart, you will know that he is going to do what you have asked and indeed greater than you could possibly imagine. Once you understand his Divine Purpose for having sent you here and his personal responsibility to you, you will rest with such assurance and be willing to wait if necessary for the desire to appear.

For centuries we have denied who we are. We have denied the work of the sacrifice of Jesus and not realized that we have actually denied it.

If it is true that the entire "sin consciousness" was removed, the veil of mortal thinking torn in two, and the Glory of God (and therefore who we are) revealed, we can no longer continue to think and act as a mortal, separated from who we are. We agree in theory, but deny in practical living.

We still hold to our idea of being a "work in progress." We hold to our problems as being real and valid and powerful in our lives. We substitute psychology for spirituality.

When confronted with a mortal problem, a "personal hang-up" we have two choices. One is to analyze it, feel the pain of it, rehearse it and try to figure out how we arrived in this mess and what can be done to extricate ourselves from it.

The other choice is to deny the mortal identity. Agree that we are a "new creature in Christ"[20] and as such "reckon the old mortal identity dead."[21] We don't need to understand the works of darkness. We don't need to analyze it at all. This only gives it substance in our minds...makes it more real to us. We simply need to deny its power and its right to attach itself to us.

For centuries since the "immortal identity" was revealed to us, as us, we have continued in the old mortal way of thinking. We think that somehow we will become who we really are in time and with enough experience...or by death. But this is not a do-over. This is not a progressive journey whereby we finally become the Light and Glory of God.

This is now. "Today if you will hear his voice, harden not your heart."[22] "This mortal must *put on* immortality."[23] We must put it on. We must choose for it. We must deal with each personal problem as an illegitimate experience. Not stop to analyze it, but just say "No!"

"No! I am not subject to this problem. No! I am not carrying this around any longer. No! I am a new creature. This has nothing to do with me. It is a relic from the old idea of self. It cannot be a part of the eternal Christ idea."

Now the old problems rear their heads to try to

make us forget who we are. They remind us of who we once thought we were. They try to get us to deny who we are and "deal with them once again."

Be wise. Be alert.

The children of Israel wandered for forty years trying to become worthy of the Promised Land. They fought one battle after another. These battles are symbolic of the endless battles of the soul-man. They never end. They never get us closer to who we are. Because we are already there. We have always been who we are. To stop and wrestle with the "flesh" or the soul-problems once again is to deny this.

The entire generation of the Israelites brought out of Egypt "died wandering in the wilderness, never having received the promise."[24] The entire generations of mankind have done the same since the resurrection, since the words, "It is finished"[25] were spoken two thousand years ago. We still want to wrestle with the old, instead of simply "denying the self."[26] "Reckon the old man dead."[27]

It is here now... and it is you. It is here for you to experience. Just choose it with all your heart. Understand that you cannot "make something happen" but the ever available grace of God will reveal it all to and through you. Just receive it.

We have a client that we met at the clinic about five years ago with stage four ovarian cancer. She was somewhere around 55 years old, had received a PhD in education, and presented herself as a sincere and warm, lovely lady. But as you might expect, she was terrified. Initially they removed a ten pound tumor from her belly, with copious amounts of fluid. After only one or two rounds of chemical poisoning as a medical treatment, she abandoned that for prayer. She determined to ask, and wait for an answer, before she took another step in any direction.

It was obvious that she would receive no help from anything man had to offer and placed her life in the hands of a very capable God. Even as she began the holistic program, I spoke to her about the power of choosing. Day after day I spoke of the true nature of God and why we were really here. I quoted every scripture, rehearsed every truth, but always ending our talks with her ability to choose for Life. "Life" defined here, is the sum total of the entire Nature and Being that God is.

By *not* deliberately choosing to know that our life is hid in Christ, and his Life is our Life, we are choosing death by *default*. By *not* choosing this we are agreeing that disease has the power on its side. This is so false. *We have the power on our side.* Whatever we choose to believe is what we will experience.

She listened wide-eyed. She faithfully went home and rehearsed every word I said to her. She prayed about it all. She read, wrote out accounts of what she was learning. Once the decision was made to trust, she did not vacillate. She chose Life.

In a way this is very different than simply choosing to live. To choose Life is to choose God. For God is our Life. "I am your Life and the length of your days."[28] To choose Life is to choose to trust. To choose to know that God is Love, that God is our life, that our lives are not our own but belong to him who formed us in his image and sent us here for his purpose. To choose Life is to hold to these truths no matter what! To stay focused on God and never turn our gaze towards the darkness. And to never, ever try to find cause for the appearance.

In just a matter of a couple of months she was disease free and has remained so for these past 3 years.

I had a very intense temptation to re-live a very painful memory of my childhood recently. I was raised in the most horrible environment, terrifying and insecure. After a couple of times in "foster" care and then often back in the family mess, at 14 years old I finally left for good. I was helped by a wonderful family along the way and managed to put it all behind me.

I determined not to carry it around. I never wanted it to determine or to define my life. And I succeeded. I have lived over and above it all for nearly a half of a century. I deny its power to cripple my mind and my heart. I had many occasions to blame situations on the rocky foundation I received, but I knew in my heart that I was not the result of that mortal identity. I was so much more than that. I was his Light and his Glory and I would live my life as that person only.

Lately that was severely challenged. I had an occasion to launch an adoption program in San Antonio called, "Are You My Family?" When I discussed it with a friend of mine from the largest TV network in our area, she jumped in with all her resources. Our goal was to raise public awareness of the many children who needed a permanent family to call their own. We blasted the TV and radio audiences. We visited the churches. We spoke with congressmen and senators. I could have never imagined the huge response we received.

During the course of this I attended classes for potential adoptive families, in order to see what was involved. During one class they spoke of specific situations, horrible situations that some children have endured. I sat and tried not to listen. I have never in my life been able to listen to such words and take in such images. It disturbed my heart beyond description to hear such tales.

But I heard it anyway. It brought back emotions and I sat and shivered. I told them I was cold. For several years, early in my twenties, I worked in the abused-children's ward at Case Western Reserve University Hospitals, in Cleveland, Ohio. I began to remember things that are too awful to repeat. I shivered so much I finally had to leave. I felt a tidal wave of fear and pain trying to engulf me.

On the way home I realized that I had two choices here. I could accept this as a real, past experience, which would validate the emotions and memories. Or I could accept this as the "sin consciousness," no matter the pictures on the canvas of my mind. If I chose the latter, I could choose that it was completely done away with and buried that fateful day 2000 years ago. And I was a resurrected son of God, full of Truth and Glory, perfect and complete. As are all the children who have endured such horror in their lives.

I chose to remember my Day of Atonement and I felt Love embracing me once again. I slept in his peace and awoke knowing that it was gone. Once and for all it was gone. No matter what picture the "tempter" hurled at my heart, I would never identify with it again. And more than that, I could never accept it for any other child ever again. My choice for them is to know that God is immeasurable Love and is actively caring for each one and abundantly supplying everything their little hearts need...right now and always.

I could have wandered in the wilderness. By that I mean I could have sought counseling. I could have rehearsed the old memories. But I would still be chasing down that rabbit hole. Instead I chose Life. His Life as my life. And I experienced my Promised Land once again.

CHAPTER EIGHT

HOW THEN SHALL WE LIVE?

Now that the Atonement is completed and we live in the resurrected Life of Christ, how then do we live? Now we are no longer magnetizing evil, pain and suffering, so we don't have that to deal with. "No evil shall befall us."[1] "No weapon formed against us can prosper."[2]

Will "appearances of evil" still present themselves? For awhile, yes. But if we see them as temptations to believe they can exist, and we choose to stand in the position of authority in Christ until they dissolve, they will appear less and less.

We must now be diligent to hold the line, so to speak. It is left for us to remember daily that we are now living the life of an immortal being. "All the old is passed away and all things are new. And all things are of God."[3] We possess all the power in heaven and earth and we must learn how to use it wisely and consistently, for it is the assurance of victory over every adverse situation that arises. "If we be dead with Christ, (dead to the old mortal consciousness of victimhood and defeat) then we also are alive with him,"[4] and we are now seated "at the right hand of God (authority) and all powers and principalities are under our feet."[5]

To be "in Christ" is really to be in the same consciousness, the same Spirit, the same Mind as we see depicted in the example of Jesus. We are not to attempt to imitate this, for man cannot by the most extreme efforts imitate this. For centuries holy and devout men and women have tried. Many still are. But the only way to achieve such a life experience is to "accept" and "receive" the Life that the Wisdom and Love, which is God, has provided.

This is living by grace. And again, the definition of grace is the active flow of the Presence and Power of God in and through the human condition. It will alter, correct, achieve and demonstrate the fullness of the Mind that activated Jesus.

One of the rare times that the mention and understanding of grace appears in the Old Testament is in Zechariah 4:7: "It's not by power, nor by might (human struggle) but by my Spirit. This mountain that stands before you this day, shall be removed."

"I can of my own self do nothing."[6] By these words Jesus defined how he was able to achieve such works and authority over evil. "As I hear, that I do." He never took upon himself the idea that the authority he demonstrated was coming from him, the man. Or that he was to be personally responsible to make it appear. In every case and for every day he subdued the idea of a "self" mind and allowed the Divine Mind to "go before him and make the crooked ways straight."[7]

This is living by grace.

In order to be able to do this one must be absolutely convinced of the purpose and desire of the heart of God concerning us. One must be convinced that we are actually called and chosen to "undo the works of darkness."[8] That this is our purpose, the reason we have been sent here in the first place.

As long as we embrace the doctrines that we are here to make ourselves "right" with God, we will never feel ready or worthy or anointed to do as Jesus did. We will feel like a meal that is not finished cooking.

"Just as soon as I get it right, I will do the 'greater works than these,'[9] that Jesus told us we should do."

"Just as soon as I feel that I have achieved holiness, righteousness, I will believe that 'As my Father (the Source of all Life) sent me, so send I you.'"[10]

That is why it is so critical that we first settle our hearts with assurance and conviction. There must be no doubt that we are, even now as we have been eternally, "one with God in Christ."[11]

This is why we must put to rest once and forever the idea that we are two minds running around trying to silence one and take on the other. There is One Mind and we are a result of that One Mind, with all its attributes...Wisdom, purpose and understanding. When we start with that eternal realization, we will then, quite naturally and without hesitation, begin to simply allow that Spirit to flow through us. Wonderful and mighty events will follow.

It is necessary to accept that we are and always have been "Accepted in the Beloved."[12] We are "Complete in him."[13] We now live in the "kingdom of his dear Son."[14] We have nothing to do, to gain, or to achieve. We are loved beyond description.
It is now time to learn to live "out from that place."

This is the beginning of living in the Kingdom of God. This is the beginning of being able to use the authority that is part of this Nature. Ninety-nine percent of the activity of healing any situation must begin here.

When the prodigal son returned to his father's house,[15] he was immediately restored to his inheritance. He did not have to wait to prove anything to his father. He did not have to endure any punishment for being away so long. He did not have to earn his father's trust again. He simply was immediately given the robe of authority, the ring of authority and the shoes to walk in that role. This loudly proclaims that the inheritance he left was his *rightful authority*. The minute he chose to return, his authority was restored. He was the prince and always had been. He was the one who was to rule his father's kingdom with grace and Wisdom and authority. Now that he was home, he needed to get started.

Now that we have returned from eating of all the strange ideologies and doctrines of men that have caused us to near starve to death, that have held us in fear and separateness from our rightful kingdom...and our place in that kingdom...it is time for us to begin to live as we were intended all along.

It is time to accept who we are and why we are here. It is time to live. And time to bring Life to this earth and all its inhabitants.

This is a very real and deliberate shift from the old thought which held us in the bondage of forever looking at ourselves. We have been fixated on our performance, how we were doing in this "journey," if we found favor with God, if we qualified for his care. We rarely had the time or the inclination to reach out with our hearts and prayers to a world crying out for deliverance. But now we are safe and secure in this new being, no more "inner critic" occupying our attention. The confidence of this new created being knows no bounds. We can now begin to fulfill our real reason for being sent here.

Once we have fully embraced our new identity, which is not new at all, how do we live? Once we have accepted with our whole being that the veil of the mortal identity has been forever removed from us and we now appear as we have been forever and ever, the Light and the Glory of Eternal Life, how do we feel, how do we act, what is our role now?

In the old identity we were forever preoccupied with ourselves: how are we doing, are we doing this right, are we qualifying correctly in order to be in God's good favor? Are we praying right? Are we thinking right? Are we acting right? Our entire focus was self-preservation, self-protection, self-awareness. We were "on trial" and how we fared would determine our eternal destiny, not to mention the peace and goodness we needed here and now.

But those miserable days are gone. We stand now

as his Mind, his Spirit, his Life. We are his Life, forever a target out of reach. Nothing shall by any means hurt us. It cannot. We are immortal and we know it. Evil can only attach itself to mortality, with all its insecurities. It cannot approach the Glory of our immortal state. We live in another space altogether now.

Here we will come up against old habits of thought that we must lose, and we shall lose them as we move deeper and deeper into this state. At first we will hear suggestions that will attempt to challenge our newly discovered immortal state. The old tapes playing about in our heads are reminding us of the myriads of horrors that can befall us. But we meet those head on with the remembrance of the Atonement and the eternal affect that has upon us. We remember we are now a part of the whole. No more an individual maintaining our own orbits, needing to find our own solutions to the many suggestions of the world of confusion, despair and darkness. We don't live there anymore. "In him we live and move and have our being,"[17] in this uninterrupted, perpetual, immutable, rhythm of the flow of Life. The old habits of thought are attempting to cause us to spin out of the safe and secure orbit of Divine Love. They are attempting to lure us into the old way of reacting, where the entrapments of the web of the mortal lie wields its self-proclaimed powers.

It is good for us to remember that we "cannot change one hair on our heads, nor add one inch to our statures."[18] It is good for us to not try to fix what is dancing before our eyes, but to look away and remember where we live now, who we are. We are not just a mortal blessed with the Spirit, Mind, and Heart of God. We ARE the Spirit, Heart and Mind of God. We ARE the Light and Glory. We live in the flow of the rhythm of the day. It is filled with Light, Glory, tangible peace, quiet confidence. This is our home and here we know nothing of the threats of the big lie. There is no big lie here.

When Jonah was in the "belly of hell" he "remembered the Lord."[19] I wonder what of the infinite, mighty, all encompassing wonders of God did he remember. Whatever it was, it was powerful enough to make him realize that he must look away from the threats and look deep into the face of truth. It was then he could say with a conviction powerful enough to deliver him, "Those who observe lying vanities forsake their own mercies."[20] Whatever his belly of hell was, it was a lying vanity, a vapor of nothingness, in comparison to the Glory that he remembered. As he was filled with the wonder of it all, he was delivered.

Yes, for a season we will need to hold the truth tight in our minds. We will need to remind ourselves of the Atonement, the new life, the flow that is filling the space we now live in. We will need to step back many times in our day to remember that we are locked in an unbreakable orbit of Divine Love. We will need to replenish our hearts with the remembrance. But as we are faithful to do this, soon the times we are spending deep in the flow of this perpetual rhythm will be greater than those few times we find ourselves spinning about, flailing about nothing. We will soon find ourselves comfortable in this new space and our focus will be less and less upon ourselves.

Now we are ready to *be*. Now we are ready to discover our reason and how to fulfill it. Now we are ready to live unto him who sent us.

Now our focus is the care of the Kingdom of God and its inhabitants.

CHAPTER NINE

LIVING IN OUR AUTHORITY

"All authority is given to you in Heaven and in earth."[1]

Why is this idea of authority so important now? Because we have been sent here for a purpose and so far, for the most part, we have been so preoccupied with our own salvation, our own failures, our own efforts to achieve holiness, we have missed the real purpose altogether. Now that we fully accept and receive who we are, a new creature with a whole new identity and a whole new perception of life, we can be about our father's business.[2] What a joy and a relief not to be focused on ourselves anymore! What freedom to have that finally settled in our hearts and be ready to move on to much greater experiences and fulfillments.

Notice now that it says all authority is given to us in *heaven* as well as earth. Interesting. For now, let us look at the word heaven to mean the realm of the invisible, where all the issues of life actually begin. The spirit realm. The world of thought, soul, and mind. Earth of course is the visible. The experience of this place is entirely predicated upon what is going on in the spiritual, unseen realm.

The Kingdom of God is ruled by a King, as are all kingdoms. The word of the King is absolute. It is not questioned and cannot be countermanded. The King is the Christ consciousness, governed by the Spirit and Life of Christ. In the New Creation we have been given a new heart and a new Spirit. It is said to be the *same Spirit* that motivated Jesus, hence we are one with him, in him, as him.

As we flow along in this Spirit life we receive *impulse*, a sense of knowing, and this is what we must now learn to follow. It is a constant impulse, always guiding thought and purpose. It is the direction and the Power of God, and as we are flowing with it we are filled with a sense of dominion and assurance. This is the only real source of authority.

The world exercises authority by position, money, status, education, weapons, physical might, even civil laws. Men spend a lifetime trying to achieve these things in order to feel himself powerful. We do not use these props. We now have access to a much greater power and influence, so we gladly leave these things behind. Now our whole focus is to remain in the flow of the Spirit of Life, feeling the strength of its current as it carries us through our days. We will learn how to access it, protect it and reenforce it as we continue to live by the strength of it.

From the beginning of the earth we were given the commission, not just the privilege, to subdue the earth, with all of its chaos, confusion, darkness and despair. We were given authority over the fish of the sea and the fowls of the air (thoughts of mass consciousness).

We were sent here to do this. We have been fully equipped to do this. We were never supposed to spend time in the prison of mortal thinking and defeat. Disease, division, strife and wars, poverty and servitude were never to be our lot, even for an appointed time.

We live by choice.

God has given us a choice to live this and every day in the flow and strength of Life.

Everything we do is by choice. Such is the authority given to us by God. If we are wise sons in his Kingdom, we will choose wisely.

Usually we abdicate this choice by default. We wander through our day fulfilling our to-do list without thought. We are choosing then, by default, to let Life flow on by without being deliberately cognizant of it. This robs us of our power. It causes us to miss so many opportunities to exercise this power.

When we do this we are choosing to live under the law of chance. "Whatever comes by and by" we will deal with as it appears! Before long we are living as victims of chance, once again forgetting who we are and why we have come. Not as mighty sons of God, Princes of the Kingdom of God.

The choice is simple. We choose to live under the Law of Love, governed by the Spirit of Life, directed by the grace and power of God, who is ministering to us perpetual safety, goodness, strength, Wisdom for every situation, with authority over every darkness. Or we return to the pig pen of the prodigal son, living aimlessly, randomly, under the law of chance. A victim of whatever appears.

So the first exercise as one in absolute authority is to take authority over ourselves, our thoughts, our choices.

Jesus said, "As you think in your heart, so shall you experience."[3] Let the grace of God lead you in this or you will be paralyzed, worried about every thought. As the Wisdom of God brings situations and concepts to your awareness, it will challenge various beliefs that you have held in your life without actually being aware of it. Wisdom and grace will begin to re-teach you so that, quite naturally, you will find many ideas corrected and therefore many situations becoming more in line with Divine Order.

Don't be a Saul, restless and running ahead of God's direction. Don't be an Abraham, deciding you know just how God is going to do something and set about trying to bring it about yourself.

Be a faithful, confident, calm and quiet son of God, mighty and strong to follow wherever and whatever the Spirit brings into your life.

The first exercise in our authority role is to stay focused. Be in the present moment as much as is possible. Spend time refreshing yourself in this Spirit of Life. I know a man who daily goes to the river near his home, takes his shoes off and lets the river bath over his feet. This is his way of being cleansed of the thoughts and conflicts of the world and refurbishing his soul. You must discover your own method of rest and recharging.

You will find that people will unconsciously "pull

life" from you, not having realized that they have the same Source within themselves. When this happens you will feel drained, tired. This is when you must pull away from all human activity and regain the conscious Presence of the energy of Life. It is always present, always available, but we must place ourselves in a position to receive it once again. Jesus did this after his busy days with the crowds that thronged him. So must we.

Another source of drain we experience is the heaviness of the human mind as it worries over every event, and flutters and frets over the life-experiences it has inadvertently created for itself. And then believes that God is the source of the confusion and adverse circumstances it is seeing. It is madness and confusion and those thoughts circle all around and about us daily.

We must pull away even if just for a moment and remember the eternal truth: that no matter what appears, God is still the Life of all and as such he holds all that is, in a perpetual state of order and perfection. But we must consciously realize this to see it. As the world sees disorder, disorder will appear. As the world sees separation, division, strife and wars, so it will appear.

We must continually choose to see out from the Divine Mind of God which is our own mind as well. This is how we begin to exercise our authority.

Remember that we have the Mind of God. We do not have two minds. Only one. But the world's acceptance of confused thinking, and chaotic victimized living, is all around and about us. This is where the choice comes in. This is what we were sent to do. As we choose to hold the truth against all evidence to the contrary, we will affect the thinking of those involved without necessarily saying a word at all.

We are God's "watchmen on the wall,"[4] so to speak. It is given to us to stand guard for those who don't know they can. It is given to us to not allow the insanity to pass by without a correction of thought.

No matter what appears, remember this often through each day: Divine Mind is immutable...changeless. He is what he is.

He can only be who and what he is.

He never changes his Nature in a reaction to what we have done or chosen. In other words he doesn't reward or punish as we have been taught. He is constant Love and Life. Just as the sun that shines...no matter what else is going on.

It is we who either are able to receive this constant outpouring of perpetual goodness or not. We *receive when we choose to receive.*

The sun shines on the good and evil alike. The rain falls on the just and unjust alike.[5]

Even when the sky is full of clouds which block the sun, the sun still shines above those clouds. That never changes. It is our choice to step out of the shade into the sun. It is our choice to partake of the rain or not. When we assess ourselves as being weak and sinful and defeated, we are closing ourselves from the sun and rain...in our feeling of unworthiness. When we assess ourselves as mighty sons of God, living our lives from the new heart and Spirit of the Christ Mind, full of grace and Glory, we are living out from under the sin consciousness. We are choosing Life. We then are able to partake of the "sun and the rain" that is always present for us.

God remains sovereign.

When we learn by constant practice to immediately stop when an appearance of confusion, or evil of any sort presents itself...and choose grace...we are allowing God to "go before us and make the crooked ways straight."[6] This will activate the Spirit of God and immediately we will see events begin to correct, to harmonize, and to appear in Divine Order. The more we do this, the more we will see the results. This will increase our confidence and strengthen our Christ awareness. We will be taking our rightful place as one who is ruling in the Kingdom of perpetual goodness.

This is really the only way you will ever have confidence and peace for every situation. Once the true Nature of God is realized, down deep in your heart, you will know that he is going to do what you have asked and indeed greater than you could possibly imagine. Once you understand his Divine purpose for having sent you here and his personal responsibility to you, you will rest with such assurance and be willing to wait if necessary for the desire to appear.

And so, another choice we make in choosing to exercise our authority is to be fully convinced of the true Nature of God as pure goodness. Without this deep and solid in your heart you will capitulate to the crazy ideas of men when they say that God caused this evil, or that God needs this evil to correct you, to make good appear somehow.

We must be equally convinced that we are sent here just for this very purpose...to be the light that exposes this darkness and diminishes it. We have to know that God is not only on our side, but has *determined that we defeat* whatever evil appears. Then we can rest in confidence that we will hear and know each step to take along the way toward victory.

Ninety-nine percent of the battle is the conviction in your heart, the absolute assurance that you can't lose. "Cast not away your confidence which has great recompense of reward. For after you have done the will of God (followed the leading of grace) you shall obtain what you desire."[7]

It takes grace to overcome centuries of victim mentality... and bless us with a Mind that knows only victory. Again, this is what happened for us when the sin-consciousness was removed. No wonder it was such an eternal event!

We must know what Jesus knew when he said that his confidence came from hearing the word of God and knowing what to do, what to speak, etc. "You will hear a word behind you saying, 'This is the way, walk ye in it.'"[8]

Trust this. Choose to trust this. Take a moment and receive this. Take several moments and receive this.

When the centurion soldier asked Jesus to come and heal his servant, he said these arresting words, "I also am a man under authority. I say to one, go and he goes. So I understand that you only need to speak the Word and my servant will be healed."[9]

Jesus was astounded at his perception. He knew that Jesus was under the authority of the Father or Source of all Life. He knew that Jesus would only speak as he was directed to. He knew that God was only goodness and Mercy and Love and he would certainly instruct Jesus to heal this man.

And so it is with you and me.

"Faith comes by hearing the Word of God."[10] Without the ability to hear what God is speaking we would be like blind men groping in the dark and unable to accomplish anything at all. Our entire success depends on hearing what we should pray, what we should know, what we should do. This is also called responding to the impulse of Spirit.

If you read this and feel fearful that you are unable to hear, you must stop right now and ask God for the ability to hear. This above all else must come by grace. There is nothing you or I can do to make this happen except to know for sure that he will never withhold this from you. Wisdom knows that this is the only way. Therefore it will always be supplied for every occasion.

When the children of Israel wandered through the wilderness, God supplied "manna" for them to eat every morning. This was a wafer that was described as tasting like coriander seed and having an oily texture to it. This sustained them for forty years. It was present every morning of their lives without fail.[11]

What does this symbolize for us? That the word we need will be supplied every day, every time we ask. "Man does not live by bread alone, but by every word that proceeds from the mouth of God."[12]

They were not allowed to gather more each day than they could eat (except on the day before the Sabbath...then they received double to carry them through the Sabbath). If they did try to gather more, it would turn to worms and they would not be able to consume it. So intent was God that we should go every day for a new and fresh word from his heart. Never try to use what you heard yesterday. Never try to use what worked for another healing. Every day is new. Every healing is new. This keeps our relationship with Divine Love and our remembrance of our dependence on God as our Source fresh every day.

Our authority is fully dependent on his word of direction and instruction. Even when called upon to pray for someone. Never reason that you know what to pray or what they need, even if it seems obvious to you. Always pause and ask for guidance and wisdom. Often you will be surprised at what comes up within your heart. Follow it and then rest, knowing "it is finished."[13]

Chapter Ten

THE OFFICE OF THE PRIEST...
THE OFFICE OF THE KING

To understand the role of a "priest unto God"[1] we need to go back to the Old Testament where the priesthood was established and defined.

Levi was the third son born to Israel and he was progenitor of the tribe which represented the priesthood. Aaron, Moses' brother, was the first ordained High Priest.[2] Their service began at the raising of the Tabernacle in the Wilderness, the place that God chose for the Israelites to worship him. This began soon after they were delivered from the bondage of Egypt, a type of our awakening from the dark confines of the unenlightened mind of the human consciousness and the bondage and pain that allowed.

While we will learn much from this study, it is important to know that there was another priesthood mentioned earlier, during Abraham's day. It was referred to as a "Priesthood, Eternal in the Heavens" which far surpassed and transcended the earthly order of the Levitical priesthood. It was called the Melchisedec Priesthood, "after the order of an endless life."[3]

This is speaking of a Priesthood that excels the human type in that it is one with no beginning and no ending. It is the Christ, and now that we have freely crossed into that "new creation"...we have become, and are forever within, this Eternal Priesthood. It is now *who we are* and *who we will forever be*. While the implications of this are staggering, to understand it we must first discuss the role of a priest.

The idea of the priesthood is to "stand in the gap" between the people and God, to make sacrifices that would absolve, or forgive the people of their sins that they might freely receive what they needed from God. We have discussed what each sacrifice represented and how that actually worked for them.

As a priest unto God, "He has given us the ministry of reconciliation, reconciling the world to God *by not imputing their iniquity unto them*."[4] Why is this important? Because it is that "sense" of iniquity, of failure, that has caused man to feel separated in the first place. When that obscuring cloud of thought is removed, man can once again accept his eternal, rightful place of oneness in life.

When the priest enters the Presence of God he carries the Atonement sacrifice. This means he remembers and carries *in consciousness* the realization that the Atonement sacrifice was for all people for all time. This abolishes any remembrance of sin which would incur suffering. *This makes suffering an unlawful, illegitimate experience before God...entirely unacceptable.* The original meaning of the word sacrifice turns out to mean "to make holy and sacred." The original meaning of the word atonement means "to cover."

There was never a question about whether God would respond to the prayers and presence of the priest in behalf of the people. He always did and he always will. How much more then the presence of the priest of the order of Melchisedec? Since this is a priesthood with no beginning and no end, this will be one role you will fulfill throughout eternity, so long as time exists, so long as there is even one man who feels himself separated from his God.

THE GARMENTS OF THE HIGH PRIEST

The priesthood had a particular order to follow and nothing was as specifically outlined as the garments he was to wear in this role.[5] By understanding the significance of the garments we find our confidence, assurance and absolute conviction that we are called, chosen and sent for this role. Garments are coverings. What covers us spiritually determines our experiences.

To begin, the underclothing, as well as the garment that covered the underclothing, called the coat, were to be of linen only. No wool or a mixture of fabric was to be worn against the skin. This was so that the priest would enter the Presence of the Lord wearing nothing that could cause him to sweat,[6] signifying that he was not to worry, doubt, fear, or fret. He was not to personally bear the burden of any situation, but to know that upon entering this space Mercy would be enough, grace would be enough, to cause *order* to appear in behalf of himself and those he represented. Any fretting was forbidden, in that it was an indication of fear and unbelief. The more the nature of God is realized, the more the Atonement is received, the more our foreordained role in this Kingdom is realized, the less we will fret.

This "mixture of fabric", which was forbidden, speaks of carrying in consciousness truths received with mixtures of error, doctrines of religions that only muddy up the waters. The priest needed to know and hold the pure and eternal truth of every man forever intact within this new creation order. He needed to know and honor the new covenant and declare everyman hid in the pure Life of Christ.

The remainder of the garments were for those priests, the High Priests, that were privileged to enter the deepest places of the heart of God. They were the ones who heard his voice, understood his purpose, and received the wisdom to carry out his purpose. Their chief function was to live as much as possible in the rhythm of the flow of the Spirit of Life. They knew God as God knew them. They lived less for themselves now and far more for the sake of the Kingdom of God. This is the place we have entered as we accepted and embraced the Atonement and our immortal identity.

Here they donned the Robe, the Ephod, the Girdle, the Breastplate, and the Miter. The robe represented the covering of the *righteousness* of God... the Holiness, the sacredness, the purity of heart. Remember now we have awakened to the Spirit and the heart of God. This robe was seamless, which spoke of the uninterrupted, immutable Nature we have now accepted, *Eternal in the heavens*.

As the ephod, girdle and breastplate were layered the priest then moved into the additional role of king, for these were objects of position and authority. The miter was the head piece much like a king's crown.[7] As we study this it is impossible to miss that God himself has called us to this role. For years we prayed, wondering if our prayers were sufficient for the need at hand. We tried to believe, we prayed to believe, but never had the kind of absolute assurance that comes now by knowing it is not we who has conferred this position and authority unto ourselves, but the Wisdom and counsel of God. This is not us reaching out for God, but God calling, choosing and honoring us. My, how the tables are turned on this side of the Atonement, the resurrection and ascension! What a contrast now when we glance back at the victimhood, the groveling, the uncertainty of the old identity. What gratitude fills our hearts as the magnitude of this begins to dawn upon us.

In the beginning, God's purpose for our appearing here was clearly outlined with these words: "Take dominion and subdue the birds of the air and the fish of the sea."[8] Now we understand those words to mean that we are commissioned to subdue the thoughts, the words, the evil intentions, the temptations of despair, destruction, and slavery that consume the inhabitants of the world, that they may be reconciled to their original identity and full understanding of God. We are placed in the position of authority and given the robe, the ephod, the girdle, the breastplate and the miter. The prodigal son was given the ring, the robe and the shoes, all symbols of the authority he originally walked away from. "All power is given unto me. Go ye therefore..."[9]

It takes awhile to wrap ones arms and heart around the vastness of this. We used to sing a song in Bible school that this reminds me of:

> "They're looking to me, Lord. They're looking to me. God's whole creation groans, 'please set us free.' They're looking to me, Lord, *as I look to thee.* Come forth in me, Lord. They're looking to me."

Now we can point to the Atonement for each need, for each person we are holding in our heart. We can realize their present freedom even before they know of it themselves. We can secure liberty for them, because it is Divine Love's will for them and our power to do so.

"Open your mouth and plead the cause of the poor and needy and for those appointed unto destruction."[10]

Following this thought then, we come to that part of the priest's garment, the breastplate, that so clearly signifies this.[11] I love the idea of the breastplate. It was a square that hung around the neck of the priest, draped over his heart. In it were embroidered twelve precious gems, each one representing the twelve tribes of Israel.

BREASTPLATE
OF THE
HIGH PRIEST

This speaks of the whole, the entire inhabitants of the earth. When the High Priest approached the Mercy Seat within the veil he carried over his heart the people, their needs and concerns. As he partook of the Glory of the experience, they also were influenced. As he stood in the blazing Glory of the Mercy of God they, in him, also stood and received the Mercy needed to free them from whatever held them in their suffering.

Remember there is one man, one mind, one son. Many manifestations, but all only one. This "one for all, all as one"[12] idea is what allows the fulfillment of the scripture, "We thus judge that if one died for all, then all died."[13] Conversely, as one resurrected for all, then all are resurrected. Since this understanding began to explode in my heart, I have accepted fully that every time I pause to realize once again the Presence, the flow, the rhythm of the Spirit of Life, I am actually carrying with me into that space the whole... everyone who is on my heart. As I partake once more of the strength and Glory, so then do they. As I feel myself being absorbed into the magnificence of it, they also are likewise influenced. It is God's way. It is really beautiful.

Tucked within the breastplate, though no one seems to know where, is the Urim and the Thummim. It alludes to being behind the breastplate and nearest to the heart of the priest. It is the Light and the Glory. Since the new creation man is come forth, man has received the revelation that he is the Light and the Glory. Remember that everywhere Peter walked, as his shadow (aura) fell upon those he passed, they were healed. As you are most cognizant of all this and your thought falls upon others, they too will be healed.

∝

In the Old Testament we find four books dealing with the lives of the various kings of Israel. Some were spoken of as good kings, a delight to the heart of God. While others were said to be evil kings, a disgrace to the heart of God. What made the distinction?

There were three things I discovered. One was that the good kings "tore down the images, the groves and high places"[14] where the people worshipped. What are these images, groves and high places? They are anything the people put their trust in other than God. And what are the people looking to as their help and security, as their deliverance from suffering, as their hope and confidence? Money, power, prestige, position, spouses, friends, money markets, investments, medicines, medical treatments...and the list goes on. We trust in the strength of our military might, the weapons we have created. If we didn't have these I wonder if we wouldn't try more peaceable methods of handling conflict. We trust in attorneys, the various ways they have learned to manipulate the legal system. We all know that money rules the court system. We have watched in horror as money bought the big name attorneys, and justice was shredded before our eyes.

To tear down these props is to elevate the people's trust in God. To elevate this, the *true nature* of God needed to be restored, taken away from the religious voice of the day. This was no small endeavor but those who understood they were called to be kings and priests by God, to serve his righteousness alone, took this very seriously. Such an achievement takes a lifetime, but it is well worth it.

Another attribute of a good king was that the Passover sacrifice, the Atonement sacrifice, was reestablished in the ears and hearts of the people. To accomplish this, the trendy, religious doctrines of the day needed to come down. The people were lulled into thinking that a particular church or form of worship, certain religious rituals, a life of *doing good*, would secure for them the eternity they desired. But the faithful king spoke only of that which God, Divine Wisdom and Love had prepared for them. The king appointed faithful priests who taught the people of the inexpressible Love of God as demonstrated by the Atonement, Passover sacrifice...for them. More often than not this flew in the face of the popular teachings of the day.

The Passover sacrifice was established the night the children of Israel were finally allowed to leave Egypt.[15] The Pharaoh of Egypt was not inclined to lose the thousands of slaves he had under his control, building his cities. I wonder what "cities" we have been building by our pain, our blood and servitude? What will happen to the hundreds of thousands of hospitals, clinics, centers for various diseases, pharmaceutical companies, medical schools, when man finally realizes he is serving a very unnecessary, unlawful and totally illegitimate idea of suffering and disease? When we all awaken to the simple, but profoundly powerful provision God has established for us.

Moses showed both the Israelites and the Egyptians the wonders of God but they never really got it. But when

God determined that the *firstborn* son of every creature would die, then they heard. And what is the firstborn? It is the "natural man," the blinded, confused man, groping in the dark from one tragedy to another. The human identity of victimhood, living under the roll of the dice. The mass consciousness. The veil that has blinded us.

It was determined that until that was dead it would continue to dominate us. Hence the Atonement sacrifice. And the slaying of the firstborn that the second born, the man from heaven might live.

The people were instructed to slay a lamb, representing again one who is committed to following and trusting God as his Shepherd through all life's experiences. This speaks of Jesus who became the Lamb sacrificed for us all. But it also refers to the condition of each heart as it commits itself to the Atonement sacrifice.

The blood of the Lamb (remember that the blood represents the life, or the nature) was to be placed upon the doorposts of each house. Our house is our mind, our consciousness, our hearts. As we commit to partake of this nature before God we are actually placing the life, or the blood, upon the doorposts, or entrances, to where we live. And as we do this...*the angel of death* passes over us. Hence, the Passover.

As it is completed we are safe forever from the effects of living out from the old identity, the old insanity the world offered to us. It is our assurance of freedom and protection. It makes us a target out of reach of any darts hurled by evil's influences.

A good king, a faithful king, a devout priest will

keep this ever before the minds of the people that they may partake of the provision God has established for us. They will not leave us under the influence of sickness, strife, division, despair, defeat, and untold sufferings. They will not lead us back to Egypt for the "help" offered out there. But they will re-establish for us the Passover. They will teach us of the Eternal Atonement and the endless Mercy of God.

And last, the king dubbed as faithful and *good* was one who ruled only as he heard God speak. He sought the Wisdom and Mind of God for every decision. He held his voice in check until he heard. King David and King Josiah are probably the ones who stand out the most as fulfilling this. Jesus, of course, did as well.

It is not as difficult to hear the impulse of Spirit or the voice of God as you might think. Just remember that the same Wisdom that called you to this mighty work, knowing that we can only be successful as we hear, will certainly speak. We only need to ask and wait. We know that God is Life and, however the healing might come, it will always manifest Life.

The king rules by his word. Once we awaken to the magnitude of the power of our words, we will gain incredible wisdom and realize the power invested in us.

Now that we have defined the roles of the priest and the king, it is well for us to remember that we are not serving a God "out there," nor are we ruling a kingdom "out there." We are the temple where the Spirit of Eternal

Life lives. It is deep within the soul of you and I that we take dominion over the thoughts, where we hear the word of God, where we remember the Passover, where we daily celebrate the grand and glorious day of Atonement. This is where, deep within the silence of our souls, we carry the Breastplate into the unspeakable Glory of the Mercy Seat, the heart and Source of Love. This is where those we carry in our hearts are healed.

CHAPTER ELEVEN

THE WORD OF POWER ...
THE POWER OF WORDS

"Where the word of the king is, there is power."[1]

"In the beginning was the Word...and the Word *was God*. All things were made by the Word. Without the Word there was nothing made. In the Word was *Life*. This Life was the *Light of Men*. The Light shines in the darkness and *the darkness cannot grasp it*."[2]

How does a word create matter? What is the mechanism by which sound causes matter to appear? Scientists have studied this. Physicists have written about it, and I have read what they have written. Even so it doesn't satisfy my wondering. I will tell you what they say in simple words, mostly because I only understand it at the simplest level.

I have for years known that every healing depends upon a Word spoken by the Spirit of God, heard or perceived. There is no Word that proceeds from the heart of God that does not cause a radical change in the human picture, or in the world of matter. "He sends forth his Word and the earth melts."[3] "He sends his Word and heals them from all their destructions."[4] It was this very scripture that I hung onto when I was struggling for my daughter's healing. It was during that time that I realized my utter dependence upon "hearing" a Word, any Word from God. I knew that once I heard, whatever stood before me denying my passage would be removed. Soon my desire to "hear" for anything and everything surpassed any other desire in my life.

"But to this man will I look, even to him that is humble and of a contrite spirit and that trembles at my Word."[5]

Jesus declared his absolute dependence upon hearing the Word of God for everything he did. "I can of my own self do nothing. But as I hear, that I do."[6] When he told us that, he gave us the key to unlock the mystery of his Life. His success depended upon it. Even as our success depends upon it.

For the purpose of study I want to explore the creation of matter as it arises from sound. When we have looked at that, we can then bring it into the metaphysical, or the consciousness of man.

We know that God is the beginning, even though Eternal Life has no beginning. But God is the Source of all that is and for that reason we call him the beginning. We find that Source is, among other things, actually sound, sound with *intention and purpose*. Intention is a thought, a deliberate thought. And thought is Word. A thought/word creates vibrations/ripples/waves of frequency...and this is the beginning of sound as we know it.

Sound is described as a "living, pulsating vibration." These vibrations "collect" and form images. Here is where physics and metaphysics begin to differ. Physics goes on to say that these images "solidify" and become matter. Words travel through the "unseen" waters of the heavens and "crystallize" into form. They say that they have isolated a specific protein that causes like-thoughts to attract to like-thoughts. They kind of lose me there but that is their story. Thus "thought" becomes reality...or the visible expression of the thought itself. Its appearance will depend upon the *intention of the source of the sound.*

In the world of matter all this might be true. But going deeply within the spiritual world, metaphysically we know that everything that appears is only an image of thought projected out from the canvas of the mind. What we perceive we experience. We actually have our experiences based upon whatever is written on this canvas of imagery. And it is words that paint the picture. Thus words can alter the picture for good or for ill. All true and permanent healings will come as a consequence of a shift in thought, perception. And this is the work of Spirit, an act of grace from beginning to end.

The Greek word for cosmos means order. The rhythm of the sound waves that come from Divine Mind will always produce order. God is Divine Order. All creation pulsates in this flow of Divine rhythm. The life energy of our bodies flows in Divine rhythm. Thus we have a very rhythmic order to the beat of our hearts and in the energy waves that course though the brain and along the nerve pathways. The internal workings of the entire system depend upon this uninterrupted order.

The Greek word, logos, speaks of the synchronicity of mind (intention and belief) and speech. Therefore the word announces the mind. "Out of the abundance of the heart the mouth speaks."[7] Out from the order, harmony and balance of the Divine Mind comes forth the uni-verse (one song, one harmony.) The thoughts projected from the Source Mind will always result in order and beauty.

But the unenlightened mind, the mind devoid of knowledge and understanding, will send forth uncertain sounds,[8] chaotic vibrations and colliding, undefined ideas and words. The whole atmosphere of the "mass consciousness" that dominates this "world thought" is full of these sounds of confusion. The darkened mind that speaks sends forth words without knowledge.[9] And the result is mass confusion, chaos and dis-ease.

Thus we see hate, where the Divine Mind is only Love. We see war, where the Divine Mind is only peace. We see individuals separate from one another, where Divine Mind sees only one. We see insanity, where the Divine Mind is stable, sound and full of Wisdom. And we see disease, where God knows only Order.

So we read that "the earth was without form and void"[10] of harmony and order. This is speaking of the unenlightened mind. And the Spirit of God said, "Let there be Light."[11] The purpose of this Light was to bring order to this chaos. Jesus said that we were the "Light of the world."[12] James says that "He (God) is the Father of lights."[13] We are sent here to be the Light to this darkness, the understanding to this confusion, to be the order to this chaos, to "take dominion and subdue"[14] the (thoughts) that are running rampant throughout the land.

We will never be able to do this if we agree with the words, beliefs and thoughts that have appeared as such confusion. We must weigh every word, every belief, every situation against the Nature of the Divine Mind. "Does this reflect the Mind that is the Source of all good?" Or does this reflect Babylon, "the confusion of many voices?"

"Acquaint thyself with him and be at peace. Thus shall thy good appear unto thee."[15] There is nothing as critical in this lifetime as learning *from* God the true Nature *of* God. Once we know him and that knowledge has obliterated the horror we have heard about him from the tragedy of religion's voices, we will then be able to weigh every situation that appears, every thought that comes to us for our acceptance, against the true Nature of God.

"Is this true about God?" If it lines up with his Nature and indescribable goodness, then we accept it and bless its appearance. But if it is contrary to his Nature, we have the ability to reject the whole manifestation, no matter how obtrusive it may appear. Our acceptance or rejection, whether by words or thoughts, is the *only* determination of any outcome. What we hold in our thought has the same impact as what we speak with our words.

Ever since the beginning of recorded history man has sought God for the myriads of problems he has imagined in his lifetime. We need God to fix this, to remove that, to create something new for us, etc. And the Goodness that is God always has responded for us. But now we must allow ourselves the maturity to see this from a higher perspective. Rather than accept the appearance of destruction as real and then go to God to fix what he *never has created* in the first place, let us begin to challenge the appearance at its very conception.

Recently the United States witnessed a disaster of immense proportions. I am speaking of the oil spill in the Gulf of Mexico. If this is believed and accepted as a power capable to harm, interrupt or destroy us, the ramifications would be with us for generations to come. Right now everyone is in a state of fear and anger over this. They have accepted it. But following our stream of thought, does this line up with what we know about the Nature of God? Is God the maintaining, sustaining, governing influence of his creation, from the largest manifestation to the most insignificant? Does God, the Divine Life, fill all space with Order and productive Goodness? Can the seeming ignorance of man, the seeming greed of man, or the seeming carelessness of man have the ability to interrupt the uninterruptable? Can we honor God by honoring the truth here? Can we hold to this *because it is true*?

When south Texas recently experienced a three year drought, the longest in recorded history, everyone was in a panic. Every appearance of vegetative life was dead or dying. Even the ancient oaks were drying up. Everywhere one looked we saw billboards with "Pray for rain" written on them. Every church marquee had "Pray for rain" on it.

One day at the height of this frenzy I was driving along the highway noticing these signs, wondering why we think that Infinite Love has even the capacity to with-hold anything. Do we not know that Love is incapable of withholding? Do we not know that "He opens his hand and satisfies the desire of every living thing?"[16] Do we not realize that Eternal Life is the substance of the very air we breathe? With those thoughts filling my heart, I re-pented for us all, for accepting such horror about God in the first place. I *filled the space* that was created by that repentance with the true Nature of God as the maintain-ing, sustaining, uninterrupted influence for good. I hon-ored it. I exalted it. I simply adored it. And the next day it rained. And rained. And rained.

Is the appearance of disease any different? Is the appearance of family conflicts any different? Is the appear-ance of a criminal mentality any different? Is the appear-ance of war, misguided political governing and the like any different?

Man is created out from the "imagery" of the Mind of God. Whatever is held in that image is perfect, ordered, and stable. Whatever appears contrary to that comes from unenlightened words, ideas and beliefs that are "uncer-tain" in their sound. The simplicity of correction comes by a correction in the thoughts, words, and intentions be-hind the appearances. In other words, "Go back to the Source!" Let God speak once again. Let his Word resound within your soul and instantly the whole situation is cor-rected. No wonder Jesus said that the healings he did came only from the Word of God, and that "Man does not live by bread alone, but by every word that proceeds from the mouth of God."[17]

God is always sending forth his Word. But are we always listening for it?

Jesus said "as I hear, that I speak."[18] Do we speak as we hear from the impulse of Spirit? Or do we open our mouths and babble words we have only heard from man, parroting whatever sound is the loudest at this time? Are we spewing words about disease, wars, conflicts, crime, disasters and the like? Or do we "speak as we hear?"

We have been given the creative ability to "bring forth" as we think, intend and believe, whether unto order or unto confusion.

We have also been given the ability to hear the voice of God and allow that only to be the word we speak.

This is the method by which we are to exercise our "authority and dominion" over the "works of his hands." Our words, when we speak in response to what we hear him speak, are the *power of God* to any situation. It is so very important that we learn to exercise prudence in this. It is better to hold our peace than to say whatever seems right to say at any given moment. God does not react to any human situation. He acts. And his action is always one of Wisdom to bring about the end result of harmony. We must learn not to react but to pause and allow the Spirit of God to impart the necessary Wisdom. It always does. It's the pause that is so difficult, but imperative.

Form can change. We see this on a negative note whenever a disease, confusion, or disorder has taken over. Conversely we see this whenever a healing has taken place. Every healing is order reestablished. It all depends upon whatever is held in thought. It depends upon us speaking only what we are hearing from the Source of all order.

I remember a lady who was at the clinic for the treatment of breast cancer. She had been through the gambit of medical insanity as they attempt to fix what they have, by their words and beliefs, created in the first place.

As the months went by she was really doing well. Her whole countenance had changed and she was showing every indication of recovering. She was happy, hopeful and even enjoying life and trusting the process.

But her husband was void of understanding and lived out from "reaction to what was being seen." (Wisdom is living out from what is true, often in spite of what is being seen.) He decided that he would give the whole town they lived in a chance to help him financially, instead of trusting in the Source to supply what was needed. So he wrote a long letter in the newspaper being sent out to every person in the community. In it he described in detail every word spoken about the disease, where it had travelled, all the treatments that had been done, all her suffering, etc. The more detailed and miserable the picture, he reasoned, the more the folks would donate.

But it backfired. Those words and the imagery they depicted were now rehearsed by every person who read his account. The tidal wave of disordered thinking that those words caused hit the atmosphere and she dropped like a stone. She was dead in three weeks.

There was no doubt in our minds what had happened there.

Several years ago I met a young mother who brought her four year old son to us for help. He had received a diagnosis of a malignant brain tumor. He was "sent home to die" after two brain surgeries, 72 weeks of chemotherapy and enough radiation to his head to leave him totally deaf in one ear and marginally deaf in the other. He was thin, emaciated, and too weak to put any weight on his legs, too weak to even talk.

But let me tell you about this mother. No matter how horrible the picture and no matter how terrified she was, she never confessed the power of disease. She spoke these words to her son over and over, sometimes a hundred times a day, "God made you to be a strong, healthy vibrant young man, and you will grow to be that." It was amazing to hear her as she stuck to the truth even with tears pouring down her cheeks. She never, ever spoke of the disease even though she knew she needed help with his physical situation. It took 8 months for all the scans to come back normal. He is now 20 years old and is a strong, healthy, vibrant young man...just as her words declared. I attribute that entire healing to her faithfulness and commitment to the truth. You see, she "sought the Lord with her whole heart" for a Word of direction, of truth, so that she would have the confidence to stand strong for her son. "In the day that you seek me with your whole heart, in that day I shall be found of you."[19]

Where did she get the faith to stand so strong? "Faith comes by hearing and hearing comes by hearing a Word from God."[20]

Too many times people try to "plug in some truth" they have heard along the way. They say it over and over hoping it will change the course of events, and it doesn't.

It is like stale bread when it doesn't come fresh from the heart of God for every situation. Like everything else this comes by grace. Remember the "manna" that the children of Israel received every morning from God to sustain them for each day? They were never to hold it over for the next day's needs. It had to be gathered fresh and eaten each day. And so it is with the Word we seek from God. It must be fresh for each new situation.

Divine Love will supply the needed Word. We only need to ask and spend equally as much time receiving.

I love to read Samuel and the story of King David. Here was a man who proved his love for God by allowing God to direct his every move. He never made a decision without waiting to hear what God would speak. He knew this...that every Word of God would come to pass exactly as he had spoken and that gave him the confidence to do whatever was required of him. No wonder he was called, "A man after God's own heart."[21]

As you read the Old Testament, you will find many stories of people in adverse situations which were beyond their ability to extricate themselves. In every case, and without exception, their deliverance came after hearing a Word from God. Every time.

God has given us *his* power through *our* spoken word. He declares that every word we speak "will not return empty, but will accomplish that for which it was sent out to do."[22] He promises that he would "let none of our words fall to the ground and die, but that they would fulfill their intention."[23]

He said "Do not ask in your heart, who shall go up

to heaven and bring down this power that I need at this time? For the word of power," he said, "is in your mouth and in your heart. Just speak it."[24]

But he cautions us to speak only as he directs us and not to "use" this power of the spoken word to further our own selfish gain. He said if we did this we would experience "leanness in our soul."[25]

It is an awesome thing to be entrusted with this authority and power. It is not for the casual observer but to be used as directed only by committed souls.

In the meantime we watch what we speak and we refrain from speaking until we know what God is saying.

This is Wisdom and this is Life to us.

"I have put my words in your mouth"[26]

"Life and death are in the power of the tongue."[27]

"By your words you justify yourselves or you condemn yourselves."[28]

CHAPTER TWELVE

ONE FOR ALL
AND ALL AS ONE

Many years ago while I was still in Bible school I ran across one of those well hidden, but profound truths, deep in the story of the dedication of the Temple that King Solomon had built in 2 Chronicles, chapter 6.

Solomon had built a scaffold high above the entire Israelite Nation so that when he made his dedication prayer all of Israel could hear him speak. He spoke of the Glory of God and was humbled by the fact that God had chosen the Temple that he (Solomon) had built to "dwell within." Of course this is speaking of each one of us *as the temple of God* and *all of us as one, living structure or temple.* "For God has chosen to tabernacle in man."[1]

Solomon's prayer was specific in detail. He cited several scenarios that could happen to the nation if the children of Israel began to stray away from God. He spoke of the various things that have caused mankind to suffer, such as disease, poverty, wars, famine, and the like. After each one of these is mentioned he repeats the same thing.

"If *one man* or if *all* of Israel turns to you in repentance, confesses your name and asks for forgiveness, will you hear from heaven and forgive their sin and heal their land?" I was struck by the concept of "one man" equal to the entire nation. Is it true that if only one person repents for the sin of the whole, that the whole would be healed? My mind went back to the "prayer chains," the long lists of folks asked to pray for a particular situation. I never really understood why people think that God is more moved by the prayer of thousands. It makes every poor sufferer believe that their single prayer is probably rather insignificant. With that thought in mind there is no confidence in the answer from God, or that they are even heard in the first place. "Cast not away your confidence which has great recompense of reward."[2] It takes confidence to "believe you have received the answer"[3] in advance of seeing the answer.

Before I go too much further into the story, let me remind you that although God gives the healing, God is not responsible for the suffering that occurs when we move away out from under his covering. Even though for centuries mankind has come to this conclusion, it is wrong and it is deadly. Remember that as we go with the flow of his Spirit, we are safe and secure from all harm. Evil may come knocking at the door but it will not find entrance. But if we entertain thoughts and concepts, allowing them to remain, which do not reflect the Mind and Nature of God, we are polluting our consciousness and we then allow ourselves to experience all manner of suffering.

Safety is in realizing and experiencing the One Mind. It is our mind for there is only One Mind. To do this we learn to pause and let it appear. We cease any immediate reaction to whatever appears and deliberately let the Spirit "come up" within our soul. By doing this the Divine Government is held intact, the problem is solved and we remain safe.

Now it was planned that at the end of Solomon's prayer thousands of "sacrifices" of oxen would be offered. Consequently, the altars were already erected. The dead animals were in place and the wood was stacked neatly under each altar. But God beat them to it. At the summation of Solomon's prayer, and in response to the repeated question, "Will you hear from heaven and forgive and heal the land?" God "sent fire from heaven and consumed the sacrifices!" This was a resounding "Yes!" from God.

With that question settled, I turned again towards the idea of "one man." I circled it in red ink. I was amazed and I was "over the top" at the realization that any one of us could be that one man. I could stand before God for any person, for any situation, large or small, and have the confidence that Infinite Love would hear and heal. Nothing was too small, nothing was too big. My prayer would be as though all the earth had prayed! The confidence I received that day has stayed with me forever and I have used it continually since then.

I remembered the High Priest that took the blood of the sacrifice into the Holy of Holies stood before the Mercy Seat and received the Atonement for the entire nation. I remembered that Jesus "became our High Priest"[4] and did the same thing at Calvary, this time for all of mankind. One for all and all as one!

And then I remembered that we are called "kings and priests"[5] unto God. So here we are, each one, with the ability to do the same for anyone or for all of the earth. One for all and all as one.

In the eyes of God, as we receive one for all and all as one, we possess the purity, sacredness and holiness of God Himself.

As I have mentioned many times, the culmination of Jesus' ministry here was his prayer in John, chapter 17. Here he prayed for us to realize and accept our present Oneness, in his Spirit and in his Mind, so that we too might walk before God as his son empowered to do the work we were sent here to do.

The truth of Oneness...one Divine Life expressed as every aspect of creation...is difficult at first to wrap one's mind around. We have forever seen many individuals with many minds all colliding with one another. We have seen all the various expressions of creation as separate entities, all the various peoples as coming from different races, nationalities, countries. We are taught to categorize and individualize everything. Just as we have been taught to categorize individual diseases, instead of reducing it all to only one thought, and that is darkness, emptiness, nothingness.

By doing this we have created separateness in our minds, and with separateness comes conflicts and wars. If once we "determined to know every man as Christ and no man after the flesh"[6]... meaning seeing no man as a separate, mortal identity with all the resultant self love and self protectiveness associated...we would soon experience what oneness really is. One only Begotten Son, all possessing his heart, his mind and his Spirit, in him, as him. One Divine Christ Consciousness, one mind, one life, one purpose to be the expression of Life, Love, Mercy, and with an indescribable sense of authority over anything which appears as confusion, darkness, evil.

Think of it! We are right now the *designated one* to stand acknowledging Mercy for every offense, for every appearance of suffering. As we move into this space in our awareness, we realize the incredible, undeniable ability we have to stop suffering, stop conflict and heal the earth, from the infinitesimal to the infinite. *And we do this first by becoming aware of this.*

Secondly we do this by forgiveness.

Remember that forgiveness is really the deliberate act of "sending away" darkness to make space for the Spirit and Truth to fill that place in one's consciousness. We choose to do this for every situation that arises...not so much for the sake of the persons involved, but that the Glory of God may appear. So that the Kingdom of God might be made manifest right here, right now. That God might be known to be all in all. The all and only! Which, of course, heals everything and anything.

Reading along in 2 Chronicles, chapter 6, I found a formula, so to speak, of how this is done. Beginning with verse 22, Solomon cited several scenarios which might befall the people when they strayed out from under the protective covering of God. We spoke of these previously:

disease (pestilence), wars, personal conflicts, famine, drought, poverty, "whatsoever sore or sickness there be."

"But if *one man* or if *all* of the nations stand before you and (1) pray, recognizing the offense, (2) repent, (3) confess your holy name and (4) receive the healing...

"Will you hear, forgive and heal the situation?" Once this is done the Glory of God is restored and the land is healed. Every time!

We have talked about how one man can repent for the whole, or simply for another. We have talked about how one man can forgive, or send away the offense making space for the Presence of God to appear once again. But I want to talk about "confessing your holy name" here.

The "name" always means the nature. People named their children based upon what they "heard" God declare concerning that particular child born to them. The name was significant, not frivolous as it often is today. The name was a definition of the nature.

Once the repentance and forgiveness is done and the space is cleared, it is now the responsibility of the person praying to fill that space with a truth about God. Every offense, every disease, is an indication that there is *some idea in consciousness which is not truth*. Something is accepted in the realm of thought which is destructive and deadly. This idea, thought, or unchallenged concept, literally blocks the flow of the Spirit.

Now nowhere does it say that we are to find out what we are holding in thought. Nowhere does it say that we are to analyze and then draw some feeble conclusion as to what the offending belief is. Many people are doing this and they simply get nowhere in their healing. It is self analysis at best and self absorption at worst. Analysis is paralysis. We should leave any analyzing to the Spirit, if in fact it chooses to do this!

Jesus spoke of "going in to the house which was held in bondage by evil" and "binding up the strong man" and sending it away. He then warns us to fill that house with truth "lest seven worse than the first enter back in."[7] This has always been a source of fear to readers simply because they have not understood what he is saying here.

The best explanation is probably by example. For instance, if I have judged another by appearances...let's say I see a man stealing, deceiving and lying to others. I see many people hurt by his behavior. Or I see a child being abused by an adult. Perhaps it is disease that is seen and believed. Or whatever I see that is evil and I choose to *agree with the evil* by leaving the person in that situation, I have then made a judgment, *without using the situation to heal the offender*. By doing this I am choking down the flow of Life through myself, as well as missing the opportunity to heal the original problem. Believing that man, created in the image of God, sustained by the Life of God, fully Atoned by the Love of God, could ever fall into disease or sinful behavior is the ultimate act of dishonoring the truth, thereby dishonoring God. *To choose to heal myself is to heal all others involved, for we are all one.* Therefore I begin every healing by clearing my own thoughts and beliefs.

I do this by realizing that I judged without healing. When I say "I" here, I am speaking in behalf of all mankind, the whole son of God. I repent. I fill that space provided by my repentance with what I know is true about God. For instance, I know that God is the Life of that person, the substance and the only essence. I know that there is One Mind and that is the Mind of that person. (No matter how much the behavior says otherwise) I am now honoring God by declaring the truth about him and his holy creation. I am not merely judging by what is seen but now I am judging righteously. Now I am judging according to the Eternal Truth of God. That which never changes…no matter what is seen or believed.

Isaiah, chapter 11, defines the Christ consciousness, the Christ Mind and heart with these words: "He shall not judge after the seeing of his eyes, nor after the hearing of his ears…but with righteousness shall he judge the nations." The whole description of the Christ mind is outlined here from verse 2-9. It is well worth reading.

This is how we heal. We look beyond what appears and declare that which never changes. That declaration is "confessing his name."

The last part in Solomon's prayer is to *receive the healing*. Remember Jesus said we must "first believe we have received and then we shall receive."[8] It is easy to stand now and open my heart to receive the truth I have just spoken. I know the offense is gone. I know what truth fills the Christ consciousness now. All that is left is to open my heart wide and with joy and great gratitude receive the healing. "And the Glory of God fills the temple."[9]

This is the ministry of the sons of God. This is the simplicity of it. And grace then causes it to appear.

This is the appearing of the Kingdom of God, right here, right now.

One for all...all as one.

❧

"And now is come salvation and strength and the kingdom of our God and the power of his Christ."[10]

"And God shall wipe away all tears from their eyes; and there shall be no more death, neither sorrow, nor crying, neither shall there be any more pain: for the former things are passed away."[11]

"Behold, I make all things new."[12]

CHAPTER THIRTEEN

ONLY RECEIVE

"And when you stand praying, believe you have received and you shall receive."[1]

Usually when you pray for something, it is because you feel that you don't have what you need and therefore you are asking God to supply it. How then can you possibly believe that you have already received it?

The solution to this comes by having understood and accepted the destruction of the veil of mortality via the atonement. All sense of lack or limitation is contained within that blinding veil. All disease, separation, conflict and struggle is found in that covering of mortality and is forever destroyed. Once we have personally accepted this for ourselves and received it deep into our core being we know that we possess all that comprises the Eternal Life that we now enjoy.

We exist as a thought of Divine Mind. That is both the Source, as well as the substance, of all that we are.

Every thought of Divine Mind is forever perfect, whole, complete, joyful and intact. Now with all remnants of the old misconception gone, we can freely accept this. We can freely receive this and rejoice in the inevitability of supreme goodness appearing.

What is the substance of this endless Life that is freely ours? One thing is that it is forever deathless, consequently there is no experience of fear. It is indescribable peace, balance and harmony. It is the eternal springtime of the soul. In it we find nothing of the old life-beliefs. There is no conflict here, but only deep abiding love, respect, and honor. There is no judgment, no condemnation, no sense of failure, but instead an unconditional realization of uninterrupted acceptance, a cherishing love that we have rarely experienced during our days covered by the anguish of separation.

And what did we have to offer to enter into this place? Only that we receive it. Only that we choose to stand still and turn to the Holy Breath of Infinite Love and open our hearts to receive it.

Head knowledge is necessary. The understanding of this provision of Mercy is unquestionably necessary. But the scholastic must give way to the revelation, for the doorway to this kingdom of perpetual Life and Love is through the heart.

We now become the heart, the mind, the Spirit of Christ. It is the same heart, mind and spirit that inspired, motivated and empowered Jesus the Christ and it is who you are. Remember this is not something you finally attain to. This is not something you finally got right. This is awaiting those who surrender all that and come empty of man's efforts and convoluted doctrines to only receive. "For as he is in heaven so are we on the earth."

As our hearts are unashamedly opened to this grand revelation we find the need to intimately experience this Life we have accepted as our own. There are many characteristics of the nature of God and one by one we must learn of these, we must come to know God as these.

For instance God must be revealed to us as our life. He must also be revealed as the Life of every living thing. No more can we casually look out at a world peopled by "others." Now we will find we are acutely aware that we look upon the face of God as everyone we see. We find a new respect for the earth and her many varied inhabitants. We see it all sharing the same Life energy, force, and presence.

God must at some point be known to us as faithful. One who will never leave us and always be as near to us as our breath. As we allow the old mindless sense of unworthiness to fade into oblivion we find a persistent presence of faithfulness. We find a God whose care and love can never abandon us. One who is faithful to his own nature and not reactive to anything adverse that might be appearing in the earth experience. When this revelation of the *immutability* of this Wonderful One we have learned to love and trust captures our soul, we will never again struggle with trust issues. We will never again make God the progenitor of evil for any reason. We will never again call evil good by giving it a good reason to exist.

Another impacting, life changing, understanding

of God is that God is Mercy. For years I found myself a student of Mercy. God came to me in the fullness of Mercy and it was then I realized that all of our failures were swallowed up by Mercy and the goodness of God was for the good and the evil alike. Coming face to face with Mercy will heal anything. Mercy is not forgiveness. Forgiveness sees error and then cancels it. But Mercy sees only the ever present radiance of goodness and glory. It sees its own majestic Life and Light. It looks upon all its formations as perfect ideas and concepts of its own making and it is well pleased with it all. Mercy cannot take in the horror we have perceived. It is simply not in its sphere of pure consciousness. When we acknowledge that the Mercy consciousness is our own consciousness, we will not see evil either and all things will appear to us as beautiful and perfect. "The pure in heart shall see God."[3] Just as soon as we agree that we are the Divine Mind in expression, and we stop to actually receive this, we have entered into a pure heart and we will only perceive life out from that heart.

But to learn of God, by God, that God is Infinite Love is an experience that will leave us knowing that nothing, absolutely nothing, will ever be withheld from us. We are surrounded by all that God is. It is the fullness of our substance within. All we need is available to us before we know we even need it. "Before you called I answered."[4] There is nothing in God that is capable of withholding. Love cannot withhold. It is Love freely expressed that leads men to repentance, to choosing a better way of living. Love does not judge or condemn, it does not give to us when we "finally get it right." It does not appear when we qualify for it. It is as the sun. It just keeps right on pouring its life into us, no matter what. We can this moment stop and silence our hearts and receive this experience and "all things will become new."[5]

When we know this we can pray and know that we have *already received* before we actually see the solution. Just as the little flower turns to the sun and receives all that it needs, never doubting that it will, so do we. Being humble enough to simply open our hearts to Infinite Love and letting that Love supply all that we need is all that is ever necessary. If we learn nothing else we must finally accept that God does not react to man. He does not give if deserved and withhold if not deserved. We receive if we open our hearts and choose to receive. Once again, and it cannot be said too often, Love acts out from its own nature, not as a result of us.

Man has been taught since the beginning of time that it is our responsibility to reach God, to seek God, to please God, to qualify for his care. But now we have the revelation and understanding that so strongly and firmly rebukes that thought. The truth finally emerges that we must simply *respond to God as he presses in to us.* God seeks to reveal himself to us, through us and as us. He is the influence that causes us to want him. We must come face to face with this realization. We must know in our deepest heart that God loves and wants us more than we want him. He has called us by name.[6] He declares that we belong to him and that he has made himself fully responsible for each one of us. The day that we stop trying to reach something that is already here and accept and receive all that his life contains, we will have all we need in abundance, even before we ask. We will begin to see that all he is... is all that we are. It is in putting on the brakes, so to speak, and being completely still and at rest that we will be made aware of this.

In the silence and quietness of the heart we begin to feel strength emerging. We begin to feel peace emerging. We begin to feel life pulsating all around and within us. We feel a softness and tenderness begin to surface. We can then look out to a world far different than we originally perceived. Restlessness in any form is the only enemy. The restlessness of mindless activity. The restlessness of the mind as we foolishly take on responsibility to change something or fix something. When you silence restlessness you come face to face, or rather heart to heart, with Wisdom, Council, Strength, Life and Love.

Our life experience in every instance is directly related to our perception of God. We experience out from what we hold in thought. We think that the problem at hand is what needs to be fixed, but we are wrong. It is always a new and pure revelation *from God, about God* that will correct any situation. This is what we must open our hearts before him to receive.

All this comes by having previously entered into the kind of relationship where you have come personally face to face with God and learned *about him from him* alone.

All too often people only hear about God from others. They hear what to believe by those who have gone before them, who have received revelation from God, and then they write about their experience. Soon another church or denomination is born. Everyone reads what this person learned and all the wonderful healings and experiences this person received. Then they try to believe it too. They perhaps know that what is said is true, but what is lost is that it did not come from God directly to them.

"Drink water from your own cistern and not another, and running waters out from your own well."[7]

Why? Because it is not an awakened revelation, not accompanied by power, unless it is awakened from within. The truth that comes from being taught is needed. But until it comes from within, by revelation from the Holy Spirit of Truth, it is not associated with the power necessary to correct, to change, or to bring a personal experience of Life.

For years I dreamed of going to Alaska. It was a youthful, romantic dream that I often entertained as I grew up. I read all about Alaska. I watched films and TV documentaries. I learned of the various animals that lived there, as well as the beautiful, bountiful flowers that covered the earth. I saw pictures of Denali, the great and majestic mountain, with all the subservient mountains that surround her.

But nothing I read prepared me for what I *felt* when I finally arrived. The feeling of it connected me forever with it. The feeling could only come when I was face to face with it.

And so it is with anything in life. Until something is introduced through the heart, the feelings, it is only information. Never mistakenly believe that going to church can ever be a substitute for this experience. It can only be realized when it is deliberately desired. When all worldly props are set aside and you are able to take what you have heard into the Presence of God alone and ask for a personal revelation of it for yourself.

It is important that we stop clinging to our lives as something to save at all costs.

Have we not read, "Your life is not your own?"[8] Jesus said, "Take no thought for your life...you cannot add one inch to your height by thinking of your life. You cannot add one hair on your head by taking thought for your life."[9] The more we focus on what is wrong, the more what is wrong will rule the day. Conversely, the more we focus and enter into the Presence of God, the more goodness and Life will rule the day.

God is something to be felt, experienced. God must be known as the *only Source* of everything we need. As this becomes our way of living, we will find that every time we ask, he says yes! Every promise of God is yea and amen! But be sure we turn to no other. Be sure we go to Source for it all. From finances, to relationships, to jobs, to health, to weather, to direction, to it all. Stay in a communication from the heart. Not full of spiritual jargon, of worn out, flowery and pretentious affirmations. Be in a relationship of love. *Keep love simple*. "I know you God, and I am safe. I know you as you know me. I am filled with your Glory as I stand in your Presence."

Now when we pray we know that we have received

what we asked for before we opened our eyes. "Before you called I heard and while you were yet speaking I answered."[10]

Along the way we will discover what blocks the peace and goodness of God from appearing. Again it will always be a misunderstanding of something about the Nature of God. Generations have repeated such horror. But to truly experience the true Nature belongs to those who desire to know him more than anything else in this lifetime. "Those who seek me with their whole hearts will find me."[11]

When we are no longer satisfied with simply hearing what teachers are teaching and we know we must find the answers from within, then we are well on our way to really "knowing" him.

The clearer our perception becomes, the more blatant will be the blocks that appear in thought. We will begin to listen to what we are thinking. We will realize when it contradicts what we have discovered about the Nature of God. We will then be able to dismiss it and replace it with truth. Peace and the goodness of Life will be free to appear.

It is sad to me to watch people struggling to receive from God. They try to follow what they have been taught and they see themselves as such failures. They ask me, "What am I doing wrong?" As if there is something they should be *doing*. As if they need to do something or say something "right" and thereby qualify for God to hear them. When all along they only needed to be still in his love. *Forget what is needed*. Forget everything else. Keep love simple. Since we cannot, by striving, add one inch to our height, and we cannot, by worrying, add one hair to our heads...we might just as well stop all that faithlessness and choose to trust. No wonder Jesus admonished us to "Take no thought for your life."[12]

Just be deep in his love and all of Life Eternal will overtake you. I used to walk a lot. I used to play my guitar and make up songs, or find the songs in old hymnals and make up tunes to them. I often read beautiful words out of my Bible, or other writings, to God. I talk to him all the time and I listen to him equally as much. Just as one would do with a very best friend, someone we love and trust with our whole heart. It keeps me actively knowing that Love loves! And it keeps me knowing I am constantly being watched over and cared for. It keeps me in a state of confidence and quiet assurance. I expect to receive. There is never a question.

We must keep our eyes on the vastness of *good* and then the nothingness of evil just gets swallowed up. Good fills all space. Good is the Saxon word for God. The earth is bursting with good. You are bursting with good. It is all there is. Only receive.

"Why dost thou cry aloud? Is there no king in thee?"[13] Stop all struggling, stop all restlessness. Choose to be still. Then choose to accept the ever Presence of an intense and infinite Love and Mercy...and open yourself to receive.

Remember that
"It is your father's good pleasure
to give you the kingdom."[14]

REFERENCES

INTRODUCTION

1 Psalm 119:19, *pg 11*
2 Revelation 21:3, *12*
3 John 15:16, *12*
4 Ephesians 1:4, *12*
5 John 17:24, *13*
6 Colossians 3:3, *13*
7 Matthew 8:13, *13*
8 Proverbs 4:23, *14*
9 Matthew 25:30, *14*
10 Psalm 91:10, *14*
11 Isaiah 54:17, *14*
12 Ezekiel 44:28, *15*
13 Romans 11:36, *15*

CHAPTER 1

1 Ecclesiastes 7:29, *20*
2 Romans 5:12-19, *24*
3 2Chronicles 6:29, *24*
4 2Chronicles 7:1, *24*
5 Ecclesiastes 3:14, *26*

CHAPTER 2

1 John 1:16, *27*
2 James 2:10, *29*
3 Job 38:2, *30*
4 Matthew 15:6, *30*
5 Matthew 9:29, *31*
6 Luke 8:10, *32*
7 Matthew 15:14, *32*
8 Proverbs 29:18, *32*
9 Proverbs 4:7, *32*
10 Job 40:4, *33*
11 Job 42:5, *33*
12 Luke 17:21, *34*
13 Luke 11:2, *34*

CHAPTER 9

1 Matthew 28:18, *114*
2 Luke 2:49, *114*
3 Luke 6:45, *117*
4 Isaiah 62:6, *119*
5 Matthew 5:45, *119*
6 Isaiah 45:2, *120*
7 Hebrews 10:35-36, *121*
8 Isaiah 30:21, *121*
9 Matthew 8:9, *122*
10 Romans 10:17, *122*
11 Exodus 16, *122*
12 Deut. 8:3, *123*
13 John 19:30, *123*

CHAPTER 10

1 Genesis 14:18, 124
2 Exodus 28, 124
3 Hebrews 7:15-17, 125
4 2Cor. 5:18-19, 125
5 Exodus 28, 127
6 Ezekiel 44:17-18, 127
7 Exodus 29, 128
8 Genesis 1:26, *129*
9 Matthew 28:18-19, *129*
10 Proverbs 31:8-9, *130*
11 Exodus 28:15-21, *130*
12 Hebrews 10:10
   Ephesians 1:10, *131*
13 2Cor. 5:14, *131*

14 2Chron. 14:3, *132*
15 Exodus 12, *133*

CHAPTER 11

1 Ecclesiastes 8:4, *137*
2 John 1:1-5, *137*
3 Psalm 46:6, *138*
4 Psalm 107:20, *138*
5 Isaiah 66:2, *138*
6 John 5:30, *138*
7 Matthew 12:34, *140*
8 1Corinthians 14:8, *140*
9 Job 28:2, *140*
10 Genesis 1:2, *140*
11 Genesis 1:3, *141*
12 Matthew 5:14, *141*
13 James 1:17, *141*
14 Genesis 1:26, *141*
15 Job 22:21, *141*
16 Psalm 145:16, *143*
17 Matthew 4:4, *144*
18 John 8:28, *144*
19 Jeremiah 29:13, *146*
20 Romans 10:17, *146*
21 Acts 13:22, *147*
22 Isaiah 55:11, *147*
23 1Samuel 3:19, *148*
24 Romans 10:6-8, *148*
25 Psalm 106:15, *148*
26 Jeremiah 1:9, *148*

Michele Longo O'Donnell is an alternative health care provider, minister and spiritual counselor. In 1965 Michele became a registered nurse and went on to complete two years of undergraduate work at Case Western University in Cleveland, Ohio. Following the healing of her second daughter from mental retardation, she left medicine to attend Bible college. During the three years there, she was responsible for the healthcare of the 300 students.

In 1973 Michele moved to San Antonio, Texas, where a combination of life experiences led her to a belief in holistic treatment for disease-related suffering. In 1975, she began offering holistic methods for those seeking relief from degenerative disorders and other maladies. During the past 40 years Michele has come to realize that there are principles of Life, that when understood and practiced, result in healing, no matter what the circumstances.

In 1999, Michele wrote her first book, *Of Monkeys and Dragons*, outlining the life principles for healing. She shared her experiences with the hope that readers everywhere might understand the possibility of living without disease. In 2005 Michele wrote a second book, *The God That We've Created*, outlining her belief that we were never intended by our Creator to live with pain, misery and tears. Further it states that disease and suffering is a learned experience and therefore can be unlearned.

In 2008, Michele released a third book, *When the Wolf is at the Door*, a "how-to" for anyone wanting to live in a state of health and wholeness on a constant basis. It is an instruction manual for living in freedom! Now she has released her fourth book, *ONLY RECEIVE: NO BARRIERS, NO BOUNDARIES.*

Today, Michele O'Donnell is in demand as an inspirational speaker traveling throughout the world. She is the host of a radio show called LIVING BEYOND DISEASE, currently heard on stations in Texas, Florida, the Eastern seaboard of the United States, Canada, and worldwide on Internet radio. In addition, Michele hosts an annual retreat in the beautiful Texas Hill Country the last weekend of each February and regional retreats on spirituality and healing in various locations throughout the United States.

To order books, go to *livingbeyonddisease.com*
or fill out the form below and fax or mail it in.

La Vida Press
107 Scenic Loop Rd. • Boerne, TX 78006
830-755-8767 (Ofc) • 830-755-6421 (Fax)

Of Monkeys and Dragons: Freedom from the Tyranny of Disease
(Book #1)

QUANTITY			SUBTOTAL
_____	Soft Back—English	$12.95	_____
_____	Soft Back—Spanish	$12.95	_____
_____	Hard Back—English	$21.95	_____
_____	Audio book—	$12.95	_____

The God That We've Created: The Basic Cause of All Disease
(Book #2)

_____	Soft Back—English	$14.95	_____
_____	Hard Back—English	$24.95	_____
_____	Audio book—	$14.95	_____

When the Wolf is at the Door: The Simplicity of Healing
(Book #3)

_____	Soft Back—English	$15.95	_____
_____	Hard Back—English	$25.95	_____
_____	Audio book	$15.95	_____

Only Receive: No Barriers, No Boundaries
(Book #4)

_____	Soft Back—English	$14.95	_____
_____	Audio book—	$14.95	_____

SUBTOTAL _____

SHIPPING $2.95 PER ITEM _____

TOTAL _____

Name: _____

Address: _____

_____

Phone: _____ Email: _____